# Avoiding the Sudden Stop

George Zell Heuston

Copyright © 2015 by George Zell Heuston.

All rights reserved. No part of this publication may be reproduced, distributed or transmitted in any form or by any means, including photocopying, recording, or other electronic or mechanical methods, without the prior written permission of the publisher, except in the case of brief quotations embodied in critical reviews and certain other noncommercial uses permitted by copyright law.

Avoiding the Sudden Stop / George Zell Heuston —1st ed.
ISBN 978-1-5008-2364-1

# Acknowledgments

I wish to thank those special people who contributed their energies, insights, and images to the production of this work: Paula Heuston, Wesley Heuston, Eric Heuston, Andrea Heuston, and Gerri Russell, Adam Russell, and Kate Race of Visual Quill, Gerald (Jerry) Shimek, Catherine Needham, and Thomas Needham.

The great mountain stands,
Thrusting shrill against the wind-worn sky,
Aloof and ageless—transfixed and still.

And we struggle ever upward—
Surging under labored breath
To ply our summoned will.

But to this grand God-stone
We are brief as shadows on the mist—
Passing thoughts not pondered—
For we linger but half a heartbeat
...and are gone.

George Z. Heuston

# Introduction

This book encompasses a young climber's experiences in Northwest mountaineering. It is about fun, fatigue, adventure, fear, triumph, danger, loss, discomfort, wonder, humor, and sorrow. It is about the old things of mountaineering. It is about working up at the Mount Rainier Guide Service in the mid-1960s, when wool clothing, leather boots, coarse-woven nylon ropes, and wooden ice axes ruled the sport. It is about clients. It is about growing up. It is about friends and colleagues. It is about family, for better or worse. It is about a young man recounting a story years later to an elder—himself—and to you.

This book is a salad of recollections, mixed, sauced, and mellowed by subsequent life perspectives and the enduring appreciation and application of the mountain experience in life's journey. Yet, the stories, set forth in their own chapters, are in approximate chronological order to anchor and orient the reader. All salads need a bowl.

Put on the old climbing gear, rope in, and tag along.

# Prologue

Dad and I were alone together. It started out as a bad weather trip: rain, and then as we climbed higher, swirling snow greeted our efforts. We made it up and over the top of Steamboat Prow, and worked our way carefully, buffeted by gusts of wind, to Camp Schurman. The metal quonset-style shelter, being constructed by the Mountaineers, was almost finished. The outer masonry, composed of native rock, was completed halfway up its walls. No one else was around. We had Mount Rainier to ourselves. BFH broke out the lunches and we sat outside in the lee of the padlocked hut.

"Good job son," BFH said. "I never even knew you were back there on the rope." We had climbed to the camp via Glacier Basin and the Inter Glacier. Our two-man rope team seemed to glide effortlessly upward around the big crevasses yawning out on this fall day. Now finishing the summer climbing season we were in superb shape.

"Thanks dad," I said.

BFH and I hadn't climbed together as a rope team, or even close together in a party, the entire summer. BFH's climbing party and rope team organization frequently split family members; and, as often was the case, with up to fifteen climbers spread out in the group, most of a climb would pass by without much contact. But today was ours. Down in Glacier Basin we had done a quick side trek on the way up to explore an old mine shaft sunk into the ridge on the talus slopes. I found that especially interesting and fun.

"We climbed up over the Prow, but let's go back on the Emmons Glacier," BFH said, snapping rubber bands back around empty lunch tins and tossing them into his pack.

I looked up the Emmons toward the top of the Mountain. The clouds parted in that moment and the vast brooding expanse of the great ice river pulled the eye upward over blue-green crevasse fields.

"Hey dad, it's early in the day. Why don't we make a run for the top?" I quipped. BFH looked up, then back at me and chuckled. He shouldered his pack, slipped the hand loop of his ice axe over his wrist, and stepped out onto the glacier.

"I'll lead down," he said. "You anchor me and bring up the rear."

We skirted several crevasses, and swung down and around to the notch on the Prow that would ramp us back over to the Inter Glacier and put us on the path we'd climbed up a couple of hours before. The wind ebbed, and by the time we descended back to Glacier Basin and unroped, the sun came out. There was something spectacular in the change. Maybe it was because we had spent so much of the day walking in dark clouds, snow, and rain. But now, with the sun out, the rocks steamed and the green moss and grasses between them gleamed with intense brilliance.

"Look around us," my father said. "There is no way any of this could have been so gloriously made but by a Creator."

"Do you mean God?" I asked, surprised at BFH. He rarely waxed on the subject.

"Yes, George, but not in the traditional sense. I think all of conventional religions have gone out of their way to craft God in man's image instead of the other way around. It is evident to me, from the splendor of what we see before us, that He is infinitely more than what we make Him out to be." Dad never went to church. Here, in the waning rain and emerging sunshine, was his church. It was the abiding experience of the day, converted in the instant into boundless existential expression—bold, cold, subtle, warm, fleeting, and timeless—a dance of natural opposites.

We talked more about the day, religion, and life, as we walked the several miles out to the car at the White River Campground. I understood and appreciated what dad was saying. At least at fifteen, I thought I did.

I looked back on my beginning years of climbing in the Northwest and realized that my trek on this day with my father was an affirmation for me of both maturity and achievement. But mountain learning curves were steep.

They were about avoiding the sudden stop.

# PART ONE

# BASE CAMP

# 1 A Valley Pounder's Passage

*Trees, bees, and feeling the feet freeze.*

"George, come home it's dinner time!" Mom yelled out the back door.

"OK, mom, coming," I shouted back from deep among the trees and brush below our house. My big gray female Weimaraner named Schatze, my best friend and trouble-partner, slogged out of the woods. I was dirty from climbing trees, and Schatze had a muddy face from trying to catch mountain beavers. They burrowed prolifically in our woods, some grew to ten inches long, and they looked like hamsters on steroids.

"You and Schatze are too dirty to come in the house! Stay in the laundry room." I brought the dog in and went through the drill, stripping off my grass-stained jeans and brown and red flannel shirt. The brown was embedded dirt. Mom tossed out a change of clothes. "Hurry, we're sitting down," she said. I quickly donned the clean clothes and used my old ones to wipe the dirt off Shatze's face and paws.

"You're good now, girl," I said, patting her. Her face looked relieved and she picked up her head, as we walked to the kitchen table.

"Tomorrow is Saturday," dad, Benjamin Franklin Heuston, AKA BFH announced. "Frank Maranville and I are climbing Mount Ellinor. You're going along."

I was thrilled. "Can we take Schatze?" I said. BFH looked at the dog, sitting patiently by the table. Her striking yellow eyes followed each bite of food from my plate to my mouth and back again. She looked like she was watching a tennis match. Dad looked at Schatze and smiled. She was a handout, and gravity-fed dog for the most part. Her "formal" meal came after we ate, when dad gave her a little dry dog food mixed into her bowl with scraps from dinner, bones and all. Such were the dog-heaven days of the 1950s.

"I don't see why not," he said. We'll take a leash just in case, but she heels well, so she should stay with us, unless she gets on a deer's trail." Schatze and the other dogs in our heavily forested Shelton neighborhood, chased deer. Every couple of weeks she would "pack up" with her canine buddies and have a day out. She'd inevitably come dragging back, often at dusk, completely exhausted, and sleep all the next day.

"Did you hear that girl? We're going to climb Mount Ellinor tomorrow!" I said. She was staring at my plate and didn't care.

I cannot recall when I began the formal motions of climbing. I remember at perhaps three years old, being carried on my father's back on a homemade carrier. We hiked the trails of Mt. Rainier, mainly from the Nisqually Entrance and Paradise side, and often we would cap the day with a picnic at the old Sunshine Point Campground. I would play near the river, get sand in my boots, and it would work into the blisters that had broken on my feet. Dad would clean me up, and we'd head back to Shelton. I had therefore been hiking and holding onto ice axes from the time I could walk the mountain snows and trails of the Pacific Northwest.

My immersion in the sport was generational. Benjamin Franklin Heuston had climbed since he was sixteen, way back in the "olden days" of the 1920s. I refer to him by his initials, BFH, because that's how he referred to himself in all his notes and lists when he organized climbing parties. He had an abiding love of the mountains, and of Mount Rainier in particular. During the Great Depression and pre-World War II years, he spent a total of nine summers and two winters working, both at Sunrise, on the east side of Rainier, and on its south side at Paradise. During those years he also filled in as a guide for the Rainier Guide Service (RGS) on his days off from the Rainier National Park Company, the private concessionaire for the Park. If there was a big rock near a trail on a hike, dad would encourage me to climb it. Sometimes I'd get stuck, and he would come and get me. Occasionally, if he felt I was too exposed to drop offs and sudden stops, he'd "rope me up" with a length of quarter inch manilla line, and either tie the other end around his waist with a simple bowline knot, or tie an overhand loop in the end and clip the rope into his belt with a carabiner. I'm glad that the leather belts of that era were generally thicker and stronger than they are now. I tested his several times when he stopped my slides or slips.

Initially I was fearless about the scrambling I did with dad. "I had to hold you back," BFH said, "and often I'd turn around, and you'd be halfway up a cliff on the side of the trail." Then one day, around the age of six, I began to grasp the notion of gravity and its consequences—sudden stops. The light bulb came on the day I fell out of the big fir tree in our front yard. I climbed about thirty feet up, was looking down at my best friend, Schatze. I tossed a couple of fir cones down at her, when a bee stung me behind my ear. I was overcome with a sudden searing pain. Other bees swarmed me, and I fell screaming, pin-balling down the branches to the ground, where I had the wind knocked out of me. Swarmed herself, Schatze took off yowling up the street, and diverted the bees just long enough for me to catch my breath. Dazed and scared, I staggered to my feet. As soon as I moved a swarm hit me again. Now it was my turn to run yowling up the street. Mom slathered my stings with a cloth soaked in meat tenderizer. Surprisingly, it immediately assuaged the pain.

For the first time, an adventure instilled a fear of falling. I had survived the sudden stop with my wind knocked out, some bruises, and about thirty bee stings. Dad came home, located the nest, and hit it with raw gasoline out of his pump sprayer. The fumes killed the nest, which was as big as a basketball. I continued to avidly climb trees after that, and scrambled up rocks, but that fall from the fir tree turned on the switch. Fearlessness was a foreigner after that. I was breakable; and with that realization a healthy respect for gravity emerged. I still launched myself off of walls and out of swings along with my friends, however. Those were "controlled" conditions where I made the decision to take the flight and the fall. It was the unknown, unplanned drop that was scary.

"Schatze, get back here—HEEL!" BFH's voice rang out through the dripping mists. Head down, my favorite hound, dropped the scent she'd picked up and got back on the trail. We had been hiking since eight o'clock, having parked at the Big Creek Campground at the west end of Lake Cushman in the Olympics. Now high on the hogback ridge that points the climber into the "avalanche chute" that was the standard route up Ellinor, we took a quick break. Though still in the tree line, our party first crossed intermittent snow patches, and then a solid covering of snow, which erased the dirt trail. BFH and Maranville followed blazes on the trees—chunks of tree bark cut out by an axe to mark a snowbound trail.

"George, we're here at this blaze mark. Can you look ahead to see the next one?" dad asked.

"Yes Dad, I can see one way up there," I said, pointing to a light patch on a big fir about a hundred feet away.

"Good son," now look back where we came. "Can you see any blazes?"

"Yes, I can see two. One is down there by our tracks, and the other one is too, but its way far down," I said.

"This is how you travel in the mountains, George," Frank Maranville added. When you walk you don't just look in front of you. You have to stop occasionally and look back and see where you're coming from. That way you will remember the route as you head back down and you won't get lost."

"What if we get lost?" I asked. Dad pointed off the ridge to the left.

"George, see that gully over there that runs alongside the ridge we're on?' I nodded. "If you get lost the best thing to do is to follow a gully or stream down to lower ground. When you do, watch for game trails, where deer and other animals choose to walk. They know the woods better than any of us, and the easiest ways down and around cliffs and rocks." He interrupted himself with a shout: "Schatze, get over here!" She slinked back to our group. "Don't ever follow her," he said, "she's a bonehead." Unbeknownst to BFH, I had come close to getting lost in the woods below our house by following the bonehead dog—more than once.

We pushed up into a clearing and traversed to the right into the avalanche chute. The snow was firm and allowed for good footing, but dad roped me in.

"OK, George, up we go. We'll follow Maranville and the rest of the party. I have my ice axe, so don't be afraid if it gets steep. We'll kick good steps."

Figure 1 The author and Schatze, 1957. We had the collective judgment of a toothpick.

"It'll be just like climbing up a big stairway," Maranville noted. "Anyway, we don't have to make a trail. Someone has already been through here and done that for us." I looked up the steepening snow of the gully and saw a solitary ribbon of tracks snaking up it.

We plodded slowly into the enveloping fog. Soon,

when I glanced back down the gully, I could not see the bottom. Mist and snow merged into a murky off-white. It was as if a giant hand was erasing everything behind us. As we climbed higher, the dark gray cliffs on either side began to push inward, squeezing our group into the center of the gully. It got steeper.

"Dad, how much longer before we get to the top?"

"Not long, George," he said. His words were as vague as the fog. I settled into the rhythm of climbing—a slow rocking step—mimicking my dad and the others in the party. I paused for a moment and felt a nudge at the back of my leg. It was my dog Schatze letting me know she was there, backing me up. I stole a glance back. Her half open mouth was unzipped wide; her long pink tongue dangled off to the side, and the steam from her breath merged with the mist.

"Good girl," I said. She looked at me with her big yellow eyes. There was doubt in them. I'm sure she saw it in mine. The rope tugged and I settled back to the slow, steep, upward routine.

"I see the upper basin." Maranville's words carried back from his pale form, veiled thinly in yellow, the color of his parka. Leading our group, he was a hundred feet ahead of dad and me.

"Great, Frank, we've got it made," BFH replied jovially.

The upper basin on Mount Ellinor, nestled a few hundred feet below the summit, was a good place for a break.

## AVOIDING THE SUDDEN STOP

"Take off your pack, George, and sit on it." I unslung my small canvass pack, took a seat, and dad handed me a sandwich. Schatze, true to form, sat down and watched me. I pulled my sandwich apart and handed her a large portion. She wolfed it down and watched me eat my other half.

I heard Maranville say, "Hi, nice day isn't it?"

"Yes it is!" A climber had walked out of the fog from above us and stopped. He was festooned with rope and slings strung with many metal pitons. This was the gear of a serious climber.

"You look like a Swiss bell ringer," BFH said. The man smiled and shifted his weight from one foot to the other as he stood. He seemed oblivious to the weather, sporting only a light sweater and watch cap.

"What brings you up here by yourself on a day like this?" Maranville asked.

"I'm just scouting out new routes and climbs," the man said.

"Well, there's plenty of them up here," dad said.

"It sure looks like it," the man replied with a nod.

"Are you from near here?" Maranville asked.

"I'm from McChord Air Force Base. I'm stationed there."

"Flyer?" BFH asked.

"Yes, F100s."

"What's your name?" BFH continued his lawyerly examination.

"John Harlin," the man said. Maranville and dad

chatted a few more minutes and the man glided off in an easy stride down toward the chute we'd just come up.

The solo "Swiss bell ringer" we'd met on that foggy day on Ellinor in 1956 was an emerging mountaineering legend. A few years later John Harlin became the first American to climb the infamous north face of The Eiger, in the Swiss Alps. He made numerous first ascents, and was killed pioneering The Eiger north face "Direct" route. After his death in 1966 it was renamed the Harlin Route. He founded the International School of Mountaineering in Switzerland. A Fighter pilot in the U.S. Air Force, and consummate mountaineer, John Harlin's life was meteoric. He died at thirty six.

"Dad, my feet are getting cold and so are Schatze's," I said.

He nodded. "The best way to warm feet up is to move. OK, Frank, let's get this show on the road." Maranville shouldered his pack and slogged on.

The view from the summit of Mount Ellinor, just shy of 6,000 feet, was nonexistent. The cold was bearing down on my hands and feet, and after a short stay the party headed down. Schatze had been active and lively on the way up, but now "heeled" quietly behind me. At the top of the avalanche chute, dad had me sit down. He scooted in behind me and pushed off in a sitting glissade. A glissade is a controlled slide. We followed the trough others ahead of us made. It was like a water slide, and I thrilled at the flying snow and the speed. As I stood up and brushed the snow off my backside, I looked up the chute to see Schatze bounding down, ears flying. She stopped, eyes wide and playful, by my side. I rolled her over and splattered a snowball on her head. She sprang up, jumping back and forth like a baseball player hunkered down, getting ready to steal a base. Dad intervened.

"Come on George, you're just getting yourself colder and wetter horsing around." He unroped me, stuffed the manilla line into his pack and trudged off through the trees, after the rest of the party. The dog and I followed. Dad was right. My feet, now wet and cold, began to ache. The aching intensified as we followed the blazes and our old trail down through the trees. Tears began running down my face. I didn't want my dad or anyone else hear me crying. I wanted to be tough, like a mountaineer. As the snow petered out to patches, and the dirt trail began to show itself, I burst out sobbing.

"What's the matter George?" dad said.

"My feet are so cold and they hurt so bad!" I blurted. BFH and the rest of the party halted. I was embarrassed, but the pain was too much. Dad sat me down on a log on a dry part of the trail, and took off my Patrol Boy boots. He turned each boot upside down and poured out the water.

"These didn't hold up as well as I'd hoped," he said. He patted me reassuringly on the leg, and pulled off my socks, wrung them out, and tucked them into my pack. He pulled a thick pair of dry wool socks out of his pack, but before he put them on, he vigorously rubbed and massaged each foot. Then he put the cold wet boots back on my feet.

"OK, George, we are hitting dry trail now. You have to move and walk to get your feet to warm up. They will. But when they thaw, it's going to hurt. That's a good sign that you're getting better. Just gut it out, the pain will subside, and by the time we get to the car this will all be just a memory." He judiciously left out the word "bad."

As I pounded down the trail the pain grew. Through the tears I concentrated on the heels of my dad's boots; and eventually, as the way softened into flatter terrain, the pain subsided. My feet were wet, but warm, and my eyes were now dry. I had come through a genuine mountaineer's experience. I had dealt with the cold and wet, had climbed my first sizable mountain, and emerged a little tougher than I had been in the morning at the start of the climb. At the car, as BFH, Maranville, and the rest of the party bantered and basked in a day well spent, dad lifted me up to the open tailgate of our station wagon and took off my boots. "Good job today son. The weather on this mountain made it a little tougher today, but you hung in there. You're not a not a valley pounder anymore."

"Wow, really?" I said.

"Yup, you've graduated."

"What am I now?" BFH thought for a moment.

"Now you're a 'Ridge Runner,'" he said.

I was elated.

Dad looked around. "Schatze! Schatze, come! Where's that dammed dog?" he said, with a touch of irritation. "We need to leave."

"Dad, look," I pointed behind him. BFH looked down. Schatze was sitting quietly, glued to his heels. She had a "What kind of a crazy family have I gotten myself into?" look.

Dad laughed. "Up girl," he said, and she jumped onto the tailgate, crawled in, flattened down my pack into a bed, turned around six times, and curled up for the ride home.

# 2 The Bush Pilot

*On a wing and a mountain.*

In the fall of 1957, BFH, my sister Catherine, and I took an Around the Mountain flight up at Rainier with Jimmy Beech. Jimmy was a bush pilot who flew a Cessna 185 out of a rough-hewn field near Ashford, just outside the Nisqually entrance to the park. I was eight years old, and it was my first flight.

"Get in George," BFH said.

I climbed into the rear seat. He climbed in behind me and Catherine took the copilot's seat up front next to Jimmy. It was her birthday. I put on my seat belt. That felt strange, since there were no seat belts used in our cars back then. Jimmy turned the ignition key, the propeller ticked into a spin, and he taxied. The plane bumped and vibrated over the ground. My excitement mounted. What would it be like to fly? I had model plastic planes at home. They flew under the control of my hands and arms with wild exuberance—and inevitably crashed. That was fun. But now that I was actually in a plane, I most certainly did not want to crash. Ironically, dad had lost his parents, Ben and Slava, in a commercial airline crash. They had gone down in a severe thunderstorm over Lake Michigan. It was their first time flying. I was too young to comprehend the loss of my grandparents, and dad did not talk about it. He never flew commercial airlines after that, but had no qualms about flying with friends who owned light aircraft.

Figure 2 A wide-eyed, round-headed, first flight.

Jimmy revved the Cessna's big engine at the end of the little dirt airstrip paralleling one of the few straight stretches of road near Ashford, approaching the Paradise entrance. He released the brakes, and off we

## AVOIDING THE SUDDEN STOP

bumped. Quickly airborne, we climbed toward Mount Rainier. It was a stunningly beautiful October day. Maple trees, turning yellow and red, glimmered up among the green fir trees. Jimmy was a social sort, and when he discovered that BFH had worked and guided at Rainier in the 1930s, he decided that we would get the "deluxe" tour. Not only did Jimmy fly around and over Rainier, but he slipped right over Camp Muir, skimmed down over the Nisqually Glacier, and exited over Van Trump Park—twice. Little could I comprehend that in a few short years Muir would be my high camp home and that I would be working there as a guide in my father's footsteps.

Looking down, I stared into yawning blue crevasses, followed quickly by fiery red meadows of Indian paintbrush. Circling counterclockwise, Jimmy then banked the Cessna over toward the Tatoosh Range. He flew through the notch between Unicorn Peak and Unicorn Sister and continued east and north around Sunrise. The few cars in the park wound their tortuous way along the roads, their windshields flashing back at us like mirrors as they reflected the sun.

Jimmy flew up over Columbia Crest, the summit of Mount Rainier at 14,411 feet, and banked down past Liberty Cap, skimming cliffs, ridges, and hanging glaciers. Jimmy knew the mountain. He had flown it for fifteen years by then. He had assisted in finding lost climbers and the wreckage of other aircraft. He knew the fickle winds and moods of Rainier, and he respected them. That is why, like all good bush pilots, he survived his craft.

After an hour and a half of dancing the skies that long-ago autumn day, Jimmy teased his Cessna back onto his rough little runway at Ashford. When he banked the Cessna into his final approach, I was looking straight down at our 1957 Chrysler, parked near the hangar at the far end of the airstrip.

The ride was the thrill of my life, and it finished far too soon; but not for sister Catherine. To this day I love flying and she hates it. When clients walked away from one of Jimmy's Around the Mountain flights, he left them with a binary experience: It was either the shortest or longest flight they had ever experienced. That was Jimmy and his "tail dragger" Cessna 185.

# 3  THE TRAVERSE

*A great view of the oyster beds.*

When I think about Mount Constance, two images stand out: the hike into Lake Constance and the Terrible Traverse.

It was 1959. BFH, Frank Maranville, my oldest sister Mary Heuston, Reed Tindall, Stan Worswick, Jerry Shimek, and I hiked up to Lake Constance where we camped in preparation for the climb. Reed was Mary's Shelton High School classmate. Dad had gotten him interested in climbing and off the street. Stan Worswick was a young attorney whom BFH had mentored in the practice of law, and who also took to climbing. Jerry Shimek was five years my senior, a good mountaineer, and to me, an even better companion. He was always upbeat, funny, and wise beyond his years.

According to BFH, "The hike into Lake Constance is tougher than climbing Mount Constance." That declaration is not far amiss. The "trail" is really not one. It is a steep rocky scramble with cliff exposure, rising 3,300 feet in just two miles.

The party reached the lake at about one o'clock and set up camp. A beautiful tarn on the rock basin below its namesake, Lake Constance was pristine and serene. Mountain goats wandered near us. White scruffy heads looked curiously from among the trees.

Figure 3 Author, BFH, and Mary Heuston at Lake Constance, 1959.

"Mary, can they hurt us?"

"No, George, goats aren't aggressive unless you threaten them or their young. But they will eat anything, especially anything salty."

BFH overheard and concurred. "When we leave camp for the climb, we need to keep everything we leave here buttoned down."

At one o'clock that morning, after sleeping bags and gear were securely stashed, the party hiked up the long basin toward the foot of Mount Constance. A full moon's light fell brightly on snowfields and rocks. We roped in and climbed up a steep side couloir leading to the crest of a towering dark ridge. I was with Maranville; my sister Mary teamed with BFH and Shimek; and Tindall and Worswick were the route-finders and leaders. The snow was a hard crust, and the angle of the couloir was increasing to forty five degrees. As the youngest, I was the only climber without crampons.

"I can't get my boots to stick. The snow is too hard!"

"George, you're doing great. Your boots are sticking because you haven't fallen. Take small steps. Place your boots on the little nubs in the snow and balance up on them."

"I can't see any nubs!" I said, fearful and now frustrated.

"See?" Maranville pointed his axe at a tiny dark shadow.

"That's no nub, it won't even hold the toe of my boot."

"Sure it will. Trust it. Step on up. That's it, George." As he talked, Maranville coiled in, short-roped me, and tensioned up slightly, to provide me a sense of security. I felt better, but not much.

Finally the party topped the ridge. At the crest of it, off to the northwest, was the summit of Constance. It seemed so rugged and far away. We took a break, and I ate half of a peanut butter sandwich. At that age I loved them, and that day, having it in hand added a touch of familiarity to what looked from my diminutive perspective, to be a dangerous and unforgiving world. It also boosted my energy. I took a long drink from my water bottle.

"How are you doing, George?" Mary asked during our break.

"OK, but I'm glad to be out of that gully."

"It's tough without crampons, but when the sun comes up the snow will soften," she said.

"How are *you* doing?" I asked.

"I felt kind of weak coming up the chute. When I was next to Maranville he had me pull his liquid Jell-O out and I took a long drink. It seemed to help."

"I saw that, Mary. If you had dropped that plastic bottle it would have gone clear to the bottom."

"And Maranville would have made me go and get it!" she laughed.

We traversed north along the east side of the inclining ridge as the sun rose a brilliant red. Tindall observed over a chew of his Baby Ruth candy bar, "Red at night, sailor's delight. Red in the morning, sailors take warning."

"Yes, Reed, that's generally true," BFH replied. "But there are forest fires burning east of the Cascades, so that's what's causing the red sun this morning. Our weather is stable."

## AVOIDING THE SUDDEN STOP

BFH, a former radar officer on an aircraft carrier in World War II, liked that old mariner's saying and used it often himself.

The group scrambled on along the ridge. Gradually the imposing summit pyramid came closer. Below it, offset to the south, was a steep snowfield—very steep, and with cliffs at the bottom end.

"What's that?" I pointed with my axe.

"That's the Terrible Traverse," Maranville said. "And we'll be crossing it."

The Terrible Traverse is seven hundred feet across and sits at a fifty to fifty-five degree angle. It is prominently viewable from Seattle. From that distance, and to this youngster standing on its brink, it looked vertical.

"How are we going to get over it? It's like walking across a wall," I said. Maranville, BFH, and the rest of our party had coiled up with us next to its edge.

"George, we'll cross it with care," BFH said abstractly. That wasn't an answer. "Stan, you and Tindall break the trail across this. See that flat outcrop in the rock over there?" He pointed to the other side of the traverse. "That's what we need to aim for."

As BFH, Maranville, Tindall, and Worswick further conferred, a hand clasped my shoulder. It was Jerry Shimek. "Hey, Georgie, how're ya doin?"

I looked at Jerry's perennially cheerful face. "This Terrible Traverse looks bad. Even if we can get across it, how will we get back?" Jerry could tell that my questions were fearful, pleading.

"Well, Georgie, I don't know. That thing is steeper than heck. But your dad and Maranville will figure it out. When I get out there I plan to ram the head of my ice axe right down into the snow, so if I fall it will be a good anchor." I nodded. That sounded like a plan. A self-arrest would not stop us on a slope this steep with no run-out at the bottom.

Stan Worswick led us out on the traverse. Tindall followed. They moved with methodical efficiency, kicking deep steps into snow now softening in its eastern exposure to the morning sun. BFH, Mary, and Shimek went next. Jerry gave me a bump of encouragement as he went by. Then Maranville and I stepped onto the traverse. The snow was pliable. The steps in the trail were short and deep, as if they were kicked for me. They likely were.

Slowly we moved toward the center of the traverse. Worswick and Tindall were nearly at the rocks and the exit point. Worswick, his body shortened by distance, was kicking each boot into the snow to make a solid step. With each kick, chunks of snow would fly out and roll down, gaining speed and volume until they spun off the steep wall and disappeared over cliffs six hundred feet below. Standing straight, the uphill side of the traverse was under an arm's length away. Shimek's advice was helpful. Ramming the shaft of my axe to its head on the uphill side with each step was tedious, but reassuring. I began to relax and take in the view. The waters of Puget Sound sparkled blue in the awakening rolling landscape.

"Dr. Maranville, what is that flash of light way over there on the water?"

"I think it's the sun reflecting off the windows of a Washington ferry headed toward Seattle."

Figure 4 Terrible Traverse, Mt. Constance.

"Wow," I said.

We were off the Terrible Traverse. The party took a break on the flat outcrop that had been our objective. I looked back at the traverse, our trail now scribing a knife line across it. From here it looked vertical.

"OK," BFH said, "there's the summit block. If we just follow this rock arm we're on now, it meets the upper ridge and we've got it made."

"Looks straightforward," Maranville concurred. "OK, Stan and Reed, lead off."

We summited Mount Constance at about eleven o'clock. Spectacular views of the wild interior Olympic Range greeted us. I ate my lunch, looked around, and listened to BFH, Maranville, and Worswick talking.

"That's Olympus over there,"

"There's Inner Constance, Warrior Peak, and up there by Port Angeles is Hurricane Ridge."

The excited conversation went on: "Mount Deception, Mount Mystery, and the Brothers..." As they looked at each peak, the men recalled former climbs and their enthusiasm grew.

"Fred Beckey did the first ascent of Warrior Peak in 1945," Maranville said. "He carved his name in that rock saddle over there."

Mountains were deep in the blood of these men. Shimek, Mary, and I laid back and rested.

"Way to go, Georgie," Shimek said. "You did it!"

"Congratulations to you too, Jerry," I said. Shimek, at fourteen, was only five years my senior. Sister Mary was eight years older than I. She sat quietly. Normally she was ebullient at such times.

"Mary, are you OK?" I asked.

"I feel weak, and my stomach is upset," she said.

I told BFH.

"What's the matter, Mary?"

"I feel sick. Maybe it's something I ate."

BFH dug a small bottle out of his pack. "Here, take

a salt pill." Salt pills were standard mountain ailment cures for BFH. Indeed, they were effective on hot days like this. Salt sweated out of the body could cause headaches and muscle cramps.

The party scrambled back to the flat rock outcrop next to the Terrible Traverse. Maranville was now feeling queasy, but said he was OK. Mary was feeling worse.

"Let's get across the traverse," BFH said. "If the two of you are feeling bad, we're on the wrong side of this thing."

Worswick and Tindall were over the traverse in what seemed like minutes. We plodded carefully behind them.

"Hey, look up there!" Shimek exclaimed. We glanced up toward the top of the traverse. Scampering happily across the snow was a mountain goat and her kid. They nonchalantly stopped in the steepest part of the wall, looked curiously at us, and ambled on.

By the time we cleared the Terrible Traverse and down-climbed the ridge to the couloir, both Maranville and Mary were throwing up.

"George, give one of your water bottles to Mary. I'll give one of mine to Maranville. Now look—" BFH turned to them "—drink as much as you can. You have to stay hydrated."

As worried as I was about my sister and Maranville, I was more worried about the steep couloir we were about to descend.

"Dad, how am I going to get down that chute without crampons?"

BFH looked up as he and the rest of the party were putting theirs on. "It won't be a problem. The sun has been on that slope for a couple of hours. It'll be softened up and you can plunge-step easily."

"Then why do you need to put on crampons?" I asked.

BFH ignored the question. "OK, let's blow this cave," he said.

The snow in the couloir had softened and plunged easily under my boots. The big steep chute that had loomed so hard, dark, and menacing a few hours ago was now sun-filled and friendly. In this long steep couloir, on this big mountain, is where my chronic young fear of "How are we going to get back?" became tempered. The slope was still steep, but it didn't worry me like before. I was beginning to enjoy climbing. I was growing up in the trade. I can't say it was in my blood yet, but I liked its beauty and simplicity. Compared to home it was a monastery, albeit a tough one. I was learning much more about myself—that I could do far beyond what I thought or even imagined. My young limits were being pushed hard in this sport and I had benefitted immensely. I was more confident without being cocky, and more in touch with the universe. I saw that I had a grand place in it reserved for me; yet I was understanding that my place, like all under the sun, was perennially exposed to the sudden stop. Reservations in life come with risk. Above all, however, was the strengthening it gave me to live through the turmoil at home, and the calm understanding that, no matter what happened there, I would survive it.

The party unroped in the basin at the bottom of the chute and hiked down toward Lake Constance. Mary and Maranville were sick but game. When we arrived at the lake to pack up our camping gear, we noticed that the goats had been rifling through it. They had eaten the roll-up strings off of all our sleeping bags. With them now wrapped with parachute cord and lashed to our packs, we picked our way carefully down the precipitous Lake Constance "trail" to the waiting cars.

Maranville's and Mary's flu-like conditions worsened, and they were bedridden for a couple of days after the climb. On reflection, BFH guessed that their sharing of the liquid Jell-O spread the bug.

"Jell-O makes a hell of a Petrie dish for passing bugs around," he declared.

We never carried Jell-O after that.

# 4 THE OLD COLD LEATHERS

*"I know your feet are cold. Wiggle your toes."*–BFH

One of my earliest roped climbs was of Pinnacle Peak in 1956 at age seven. Pinnacle is a sharp triangular peak in Mount Rainier's Tatoosh Range, overlooking Reflection Lake. The rope we used wasn't made for climbing. It was just a thirty-foot length of quarter-inch manila line that BFH tied me into with a French bowline knot. My boots were leather but not built for climbing either. In that era they were known as Patrol Boy boots. I don't know who made them, but they were rugged and had steel toes. My feet were OSHA-approved. The soles were softer than Vibrams but stuck well to the dry basalt rock on that sunny autumn day. Only Dad and I were on that scramble. On the way back and before we unroped, BFH took my picture in the Pinnacle saddle.

"You take to this," Dad said as we sat eating our lunch. He playfully reached out and cracked a hard-boiled egg on my head.

In 1960, before the serious climbing season began, BFH bought me my first pair of climbing boots. They were a good brand for the time, with Vibram soles, but their stiff leather caused blisters. Blisters, however, were merely part of "breaking in the boots." Some did this by standing in a water-filled bathtub, which loosened the leather and formed it to the foot. I did it by wearing the boots on hikes and climbs. The boots broke me in. Occasionally BFH worked them over with a rubber hammer to soften the leather, especially around the heels, where most blisters persisted. Our old boots were topped with nylon waterproof gaiters for glacier climbs.

BFH would grease and SnoSeal our climbing boots. Sometimes he would swab on silicone liquid. Special care was taken to waterproof all stitching and seams. No matter how much waterproofing was applied, however, leather climbing boots rarely went a full day in the snow and slush without becoming wet. Wet meant cold. The insulating properties of these single-shell leather climbing boots were marginal. If you kept moving, they could be warm enough; friction from walking generated heat. But when you stopped, cold quickly crept in.

## AVOIDING THE SUDDEN STOP

My feet were chronically cold in the old leather boots. However, in 1968 I bought a pair of high-altitude expedition boots that I kept at the Camp Muir guide hut for summit days. These were black chrome-tanned waterproof leather with a triple boot. The inner bootie was felt; a middle leather lace-up "shoe" insert went over the felt, and that felt-shoe combination in turn slipped into the rigid lace-up outer shell. These boots were bulky and heavy, but transformed my climbing experience. They required no breaking in, and they were warm and extremely comfortable. It is amazing to me how much properly warmed feet (and hands) diminished the overall stress of the sport.

Figure 5 On the trail in to Little Tahoma, 1961, wearing the old cold leather boots. The summit of Little Tahoma is at the upper left.

The old cold leather boots of the early days were also heavy in proportion to my stamina. I was small for my age in the early '60s. Lifting boots thousands of times in the course of a climb sometimes had frustrating consequences. Hiking back down the trail from Summerland after summiting Little Tahoma in 1961, I was so tired that I could not lift my feet over tree roots. I saw the roots, whose gnarled shapes were only three inches above the smoother surface of the trail, but for the life of me, I could neither raise nor will my climbing boots over them. Half a dozen times, in the last four miles out to the trailhead, I tripped and sprawled headlong over those infernal roots. They became alive—cunning, waiting, grasping. BFH pulled me back to my feet and dusted me off. A switchback or two later I would trip again. Dad picked me up and dusted me off again.

"Dad, I can't get my feet over them!" I sobbed.

"Let's take a break." BFH stopped next to a stream tumbling under a tiny bridge on the trail. "Take that tin cup off the back of my pack." I handed it to him. He reached upstream, filled the cup, and handed it back. In those days you could safely drink the water. It was the coldest, sweetest water I'd ever tasted. We sat, drank from the cup, and rested. We didn't speak, just listened to the bubbling stream, and watched the late afternoon light arrayed among the giant trees. I understood again that I was among friends, just like in my woods at home with my dog: no hard feelings. It was the way of the woods, and I was being reminded of my place in it. I calmed down, and dozed off.

"OK, time to head for the car, George," BFH said, slowly standing up. I startled awake. "Grab hold of my pack and hang on. We'll go slower."

I knew we must be nearing the parking lot and the

end of the trail. Rounding each bend I anticipated it; but the trail went on endlessly. Finally I could hear sounds of cars on the road. I focused on those sounds—the audible confirmation that my climb of Little Tahoma was finished; and presaged green grass, my dog Schatze, and the home that now lay at the far end of the asphalt ribbon those cars were using. Schatze couldn't make the climb. It was too tough and exposed, and anyway, she wasn't allowed in Rainier National Park without a leash. Schatze didn't like leashes, and none of us was going to climb trying to hang onto one.

The heavy leather climbing boots, with me still in them, finally made it to the trailhead.

"Way to go, Georgie!" Jerry Shimek smiled from his seat on the tailgate of our car, "you did it!"

"Thanks Jerry," I heard myself mutter. I wearily doffed my pack, ice axe, and boots, climbed into the back seat, and fell asleep.

## 5  THE GREASE

*"Let's grab a burger at the next drive-in."* –BFH

My dad's words floated me awake. I remembered that I had just made it off Little Tahoma.

"There's an Arctic Circle drive-in over there on the left, Mr. Heuston," I heard Shimek say. I felt the car slow down and make a hard left turn, and I forced myself to sit up. We stopped. BFH, Maranville, and Shimek got out, so I did as well—or tried to. My legs had stiffened into a sitting position, and they ached in protest as I exited the car. My muscles slowly uncoiled, allowing me to stand stooped. Dad was at the window with Shimek and Maranville ordering.

"I'll have a double meat, double cheese burger with everything on it," he said.

"Anything else sir?" A female voice floated back out

the window.

"Yes, I'd like a chocolate marshmallow malt milkshake," he paused, "and throw in a side of onion rings."

"George, do you want the same?" I nodded as I hobbled over to the picnic table under the outside awning. "Make that two orders," he said to the hidden clerk inside.

"All the same?" she said.

"Yup," BFH said.

The four of us sat at the picnic table unwrapping the oil-soaked coverings of our hamburgers. No words were spoken through the first bites. My double meat, double cheese burger looked like a mountain. Lettuce, onions, pickles, meat, buns, cheese, ketchup, and mayonnaise, all combined sublimely into a warm, happy, melted mass. I picked it up with both hands and took a bite, struggling to get my mouth over the concoction. As I bit down, a warm tan and red liquid of blended ingredients and grease ran in rivulets down my bare arms and dripped off my elbows.

"Now that's a burger," BFH said approvingly. He was already halfway through his. Maranville left the table and came back with a fist full of paper napkins.

"What did you think of the ranger when we checked out from the climb?" Shimek asked BFH. "He didn't believe our group had actually climbed Little Tahoma. He kept saying that nobody had made it up to the summit yet this year, but we did it!"

"We sure did," Maranville smiled, wiping his mouth after his last bite of burger.

"Yes, we did," concurred dad, a hint of pride in his voice. "Those rangers manning the park entrances don't get into the back country, let alone on the mountain or any of the peaks. They're summer temporary employees, and don't drift far from their coffee cups.

BFH stood up. "OK, let's hit the road. George and Jerry, you can take your shakes and drink them in the car." I could see that BFH's legs were stiff too. He slowly walked over and dumped the lunch effluvia into the trash can, and pulled the car keys out of his pocket. "Damned good burger," he said.

The dyspepsia experienced on the rest of the drive home neutralized the aches and exhaustion of the trail. Grease and milkshakes became a post-climb ritual.

## 6 Walking on fire

*"I know you're growing, but you'll have to wear these another season." –BFH*

When I was fourteen my body decided to grow, but my boots didn't. The year before, in 1962, dad drove me up to the Recreational Equipment Inc. store in Seattle. He fitted me into new expensive leather climbing boots, and bought a set of crampons to go with them.

"Gary, let's fit these boots on the large side. I think George is going to grow this year." REI Manager Gary Rose, a former Rainier Guide Service guide, and friend of the family, disappeared into the back room. He came out with a set of new leathers.

"Let's try these on you George." They were more rigid, insulated, and made in Austria. I walked around the store. They felt good there, of course, so BFH bought them. But out on the trail, their stiffness caused severe blisters. It took the entire climbing season of 1963 to break them in, but by the fall of that year they finally became comfortable. I grew six inches between that fall and the beginning of the next climbing season in May, and kept growing. The boots were tolerable for wear on the climb of Mount Saint Helens, but on the way down my toes started jamming in the boots. The next climb was Mount Adams.

Again my boots functioned well on the climb up, but going downhill my toes pounded on the fronts. Descending decayed into flinching steps, each more painful than the last. I limped into high camp, where BFH and the rest of the party were busily preparing to leave.

"Dad, I can't take these boots. They're jamming my toes and are really painful."

"I could take a look at them George, but at this point you don't have any alternative but to wear them. It's only a few miles out to the car, so you're going to have to gut it out."

We packed up, dropped down over the snowfield below camp, and regained the trail into the tree line. On snow, I was able to plunge my boots and dampen the pain, but on dry hard ground, they came at me with a vengeance. I had tried tying the tops of my boots as tight as I could to keep my feet from sliding forward against the toes, but that didn't work because there was no room to slide. My feet had simply grown too large, and the hard unyielding leather was acting like a hammer against them.

The pain came in waves. At times, I felt that I could "gut it out," and met some success in locking each searing step into its own room in the back of my brain. But inexorably the torment returned. I found that canting my boots and walking on their outside edges slightly mitigated my misery. But in a few hundred feet my ankles began to hurt. By now my toes were on fire. It was a fire relit with each step. I decided that there was no point in sitting down and taking off my boots. I needed to hike through this and get to the car. It seemed as though the trail out was twice as long as it was on the way in— but finally, I hobbled out to the trailhead. I dropped my pack on the tailgate of the car and sat down on a rock. I could now tend to my throbbing feet. BFH stood by. I slid off my socks and boots. My toes were covered in blood.

"Your toenails have been lifted up," BFH said, taking a foot in his hand. He grabbed his first aid kit applied some cream from a tube, and wrapped my toes in gauze, then did the same with the other foot. He slid a pair of clean socks over them.

The next week BFH and I drove back up to REI in Seattle. We returned to Shelton with a new pair of climbing boots with plenty of toe room. My feet had grown two sizes, so BFH fitted me two sizes higher to accommodate growth.

I reflected often on my fire-walking experience. Why

did dad ignore my plight? It was not as if I grew two sizes overnight. I had complained about the old boots often on climbs that year. Somehow, however, it didn't register. BFH was a tough old bird— and it took sacrifice of blood and pain to convince him that I needed a pair of larger boots— now. He was also a product of the Great Depression, where things bought were coveted and kept. Whatever the reasons, the conclusion of climbing summer of 1963 was a long walk on fire.

# 7 THE CLOTHES

*"You can go a hell of a long way on boiled wool."*
–BFH

In the pre-fleece era of the '60s, wool ruled mountaineering. Because of my father's influence, I preferred thick wool knicker pants. They buckled just below the knees and provided excellent unrestricted movement. Heavy wool knicker socks, worn over wool-blend long johns, completed the waist-down glacier climbing kit. Wool shirts were worn up top. Every year, BFH and I would drive down to the Pendleton Woolen Mill store in Washougal, Washington, on the Columbia River, east of Vancouver. There we would select the "blems," the shirts with ever-so-slight defects. They could be bought for a song and made peerless garments for climbing.

BFH and my mom, Ruth, fought frequently. When

Mom got really mad at BFH, she'd run his Pendletons through the wash and dry them on high heat. They'd shrink. Unfortunately for BFH, he could no longer use them. Fortunately for me, I could.

When we made our trips up to Recreational Equipment Inc. (REI) in Seattle to buy climbing ropes, web sling nylon, and carabiners, BFH would grab several pairs of English wool mittens. He bought them extra-large, and when he got home he boiled them in a big pot on the stove to shrink them. He stank up the kitchen, and Mom got mad, but that did not deter him. He threw them into the clothes dryer set on high, pulled them out, and boiled them again. After three or four boiling and drying cycles, the weave of the mittens became so tight that it shed water. At this point BFH considered the job done. The mittens were worn with snug-fitting light unboiled wool gloves underneath. This comprised the layered approach to clothing that worked so well in the Northwest. Boiled

Figure 6 Sporting one of BFH's shrunken yellow Pendleton shirts on the Muir Snowfield.

wool mittens were remarkable—warm and windproof. Even when wet they retained heat, and their rough texture allowed for a good grip on an ice axe or rope. If the weather was particularly cold, large leather overmittens could top off the combination.

The rough textures of wool appealed to BFH for a reason. They retarded falls. If he slipped and had to self-arrest, his wool knickers grabbed the snow and slowed acceleration. On several occasions, when our party approached a dicey steep section on a glacier, BFH would not let the group continue until everyone had taken off their nylon wind pants. "If you wear nylon on steep snow or ice, you might as well grease your butt," BFH opined. He was right. Wool was Velcro and nylon was Teflon when it came to taking falls. The difference could mean life or death.

The Pendleton wool shirts were followed with a wool sweater-vest or down vest as bad weather dictated. In 1960, BFH bought himself and me Gerry down vests. He liked down, provided a shell parka was worn over it to keep it dry and retain its insulating properties. The Gerry vests proved essential. They were light, stuffed easily anywhere in the pack, and made good pillows in a bivouac.

"These vests keep the core heat in while keeping freedom of movement in the arms," BFH observed.

BFH meticulously laid out his clothes before a climb. He would roll each item tightly, rubber-band it, and put it into a plastic sack for packing, which he in turn rubber banded. He took extra wool socks. He liked Maurice Herzog's solution on Annapurna in 1952: When Herzog lost his gloves, he put his extra pair of socks on his hands. No matter that Maurice later lost all his fingers from frostbite; it was a good idea. I followed BFH in organizing my pack and clothing until I started guiding with the RGS.

I discovered in the RGS that I was in and out of my pack so much on behalf of myself and clients, that it was not feasible to take the time to return items to their separate sacks. My solution was to open an extra-large garbage sack, line the inside of my big Kelty frame pack with it, and stuff all my clothes in. But there was a trick to it. I packed every item, from sweaters to parka shells, with one sleeve sticking up. When I needed a garment, I'd just grab its sleeve and pull with one hand while holding everything else in with the other. It worked like a charm. I still kept any down-filled items, like my Thaw parka and Gerry vest in separate waterproof stuff sacks; I could not afford to get them wet. The down gear was most effective above ten thousand feet, away from wet snow and rain, so we stored most of it in the guide hut at Muir.

We dried all our gear back at the RGS store and rental space in the basement of the Henry M. Jackson Visitor's Center, a.k.a. "The DUB" (Day Use Building). The wet leather boots were dried in front of a big heater, with laces tied together so pairs would not be mixed. Wool garb was put into a big industrial washing machine, washed in Ivory Flakes in cold water and then thrown into the dryer on air dry. Sometimes sweaters were hand-washed and then dried in the room with the boots.

My trusty boiled wool gloves were treated like normal attire; they were washed in the machine in hot water and tossed into the dryer on hot. It just made them better.

"George, put your boots up on top of the water heater."

Dad and I were cleaning out the car after a particularly wet outing. We had just returned from a climb of Mount Thorson in the Olympics. Much of the trip involved fighting through wet brush and Devil's Club. Oplopanax horridus, grows tall with a woody stalk. It is strong enough to catch a slip on steep slopes, but there's a price—the stalk is graced with long needle-like thorns that can penetrate leather gloves. Hence the Latin "horridus." I reached into the car to grab my boots, and my forearm brushed past my leather gloves.

"Ow!"

"What's the matter?" BFH asked, more out of interest than concern.

"I got stuck again with a devil's club thorn," I said, irritated.

"The damned things go through just about anything. Toss the gloves out on the garage floor. I'll get them cleaned out," BFH said.

I set my saturated climbing boots on the basement water heater next dad's gear. The low heat radiating from the top of the tank would dry them in twelve hours. BFH took my thick leather gloves to his workbench, grabbed a set of needle nosed pliers and carefully pulled the devil's club spines out, slowly turning the pliers to keep from breaking the wicked points off.

"Looks like I got them all," he said, tossing me the gloves. I threw them up on top of my boots to dry. In the Olympics, the proliferation of devil's club required tough leather gloves in order to negotiate any off-trail approaches to climbs. Prehistoric in appearance, Oplopanax horridus earned my grudging respect. It liked growing on old rock slides at the base of cliffs, and would even propagate its way up steep draws—all the places we needed to go. It was a primary factor in my preference for climbing in the Cascades. The dreaded devil's club wasn't over there.

8  THE AXE

*A first turn with an ice axe.*

In May 1959, at age nine, I was allowed to use an ice axe for the first time on a climb of Mount Washington in the Olympics. I had not yet been instructed on how to use it to self-arrest. It had a leather safety scabbard on it, and BFII would not let me take it off until he was satisfied that I was going to carry it responsibly. He eyed me with approval as we hiked in on the long approach to the mountain from the Big Creek trailhead near Lake Cushman. I was walking with my hand over the top, pick pointed backward and thumb under the adz in accepted American mountaineering fashion. We scrambled up through the tree line approaching Mount Washington's eastern face, which was our route for the day.

BFH finally said, "OK, George, go ahead and take

the cover off." It was now hands on bare steel—finally.

"Schatze, come, heel!" Dad called.

My dog broke off a scent trail and darted out of the trees of the steep ridge, and swung into line behind me, her long pink tongue dangling. She was a veteran mountaineer now, having been on every climb with us in the Olympics since we were baptized in the sport on Mount Ellinor several years ago. She now knew how to measure her strength, and true to her breed, she intended to use it all up. By the end of the climb she would be plodding wearily, placidly, by my side, anticipating, as I was, the joy of reaching the car.

On that crisp, sunny day, our party traversed west off of a ridge into a snow-filled gully or couloir, with BFH and me roped together. Normally climbers from the same family were not, to mitigate potential multiple losses in case of tragic sudden stops. As we trudged upward, BFH kicked steps in the hard snow, and little marbles of it skittered down and past me. The ice axe fit well in my hand by now, and I enjoyed the extra balance it provided. The couloir angled up into a snow bowl, where we rested. Above the bowl another snow couloir angled hundreds of feet up into rock buttresses under Washington's summit pyramid, named after George Washington because the peak resembled the reclining profile of the president's head. The party climbed the couloir and began a short left-hand traverse to gain access to the summit ridge. The snow was now loosened by the sun. BFH coiled me in next to him. I jammed the shaft of my axe and hit a rock. I pulled it out and thrust it in harder.

"Ow! What are you doing?" BFH's voice was a mixture of pain and irritation. "That's my boot you're sticking me with!"

"Sorry, Dad." At least I knew the point was sharp.

Figure 7 Near the summit of Mount Washington prior to BFH's fall.

We summited, signed the register, had lunch, and headed down the standard route. This entailed descending the summit pyramid's southeastern side. Schatze didn't like the cliffs and exposure. She barked in protest. At the base of the pyramid, the route skirted down to the east on a steep snow-covered ledge. The ledge was perhaps fifteen-feet-wide, and its low end abutted a cliff several hundred-feet-high. I was in front climbing down with BFH anchoring the rope from behind. There was a soft *whoosh*. I turned to see BFH sliding on his rear end toward the edge of the cliff. He had a surprised look on his face and was picking up speed rapidly. He was not self-arresting, and soon he would be past me. It was now time for me to be surprised. Instantly time slowed. I thought, "If I don't do something right now, dad will go over the cliff and me with him. He isn't responding."

I recalled the cliff he was headed for. I had looked across at it on the way up. It was vertical, several hundred feet high, and terminated at a boulder and snow basin. I didn't want to die young, and right there. But what to do? I was surprised how clear my thoughts ran. No panic–but there was precious little time no matter how it slowed and I was aware of that. Something had to be done if we were going to live through this, and it was going to have to be done with what was at hand– my ice axe.

I lifted the shaft of my axe completely out of the snow grabbed the rope, took one turn around the shaft, drove it back into the snow down to its head, and put all my weight on it. I prayed that the axe would not pull out. I was staring so hard at it that I could see the small pitting and rust marks on the adz of the axe. After what seemed an interminable wait, the rope snapped tight. The axe didn't budge. I glanced down at BFH. He was snugged up just short of the cliff. His boots were no more than ten feet from a very long drop. I looked back up the eighty feet of slide marks to where his fall had begun.

He had taken a "leader fall." These are the most dangerous kind, because if a climber leading an ascending rope team slips, he will fall twice the distance of the rope before his next rope-mate has a chance to stop it. This is doubly dangerous. On a descent, the leader of the rope anchors it for his team, so normally the strongest and most experienced climber is at the tail end. But if he falls, he again goes twice the distance.

I was afraid to look up. I felt like I had to keep staring at the axe and pressing down on it or it would evaporate into thin air, and I would find myself pulled inexorably toward the ragged edge of the cliff, my father's body, already over it and falling freely, accelerating mine. A father and son meet death together on Mount Washington. Now I was afraid, shaking.

BFH slowly stood up and brushed off the snow and slush.

"Thanks," he said. "You saved me."

"Dad, I didn't save you, I saved me!" I heard myself retort. He thought for a minute and nodded. He saw me shaking.

"OK," BFH said, clearing his throat. "Let's move around the corner and catch up with Maranville's rope." It was a sudden stop avoided, and I had my now trusty axe to thank for it, along with an instant self-taught course on how to set an ice-axe belay. As we walked off the ledge and cleared a corner, Schatze was sitting, patiently waiting for us. What would she have done if we had not shown up? Likely she would have wandered back to look for us, and Maranville and the rest of the party, not seeing man, boy, or dog emerge from the trail above, would have climbed back up to look. They would have seen the slide marks over the cliff, my dog sitting on the edge, looking over. I envisioned her howling sorrowfully. The thought put a lump in my throat.

The heat of the afternoon turned the snow soft. It plunged with each downward step. Wet balls of it dislodged from our feet, gained momentum, and rolled into ever larger balls, picking up snow and making little tracks, until they wobbled to a stop a hundred feet below. We gained the tree line and the trail, and walked to the car. Dad never mentioned his fall to Maranville or anyone else in the party. I had a hard time taking off my boots. My hands were shaking as I again mulled possible consequences of the event. But I was back on kinder ground, and I thanked my shoulder angel. I had avoided the sudden stop.

"Come here, girl," I said, patting my leg. Schatze jumped onto the tailgate and sat next to me. Somehow she understood. "I love you, girl." I whispered the words softly in her ear. Life suddenly seemed sharper, more real—the feel of her short silky coat and the warmth of her big gray body against mine—loving, consoling, celebrating. We were together here. We were together now.

Several decades later as BFH lay dying of pancreatic cancer at age ninety-four, he reflected with me on the

*AVOIDING THE SUDDEN STOP*

incident.

"So you did a self-arrest?" he said.

"No, Dad, you hadn't taught me that yet."

BFH nodded weakly. "I guess not. Then how did you stop me?"

"I took a turn of the rope around the shaft of my ice axe and drove it into the snow. You got a static belay."

"Where did you learn to do that?"

"On Mount Washington in 1960," I said.

He chuckled softly.

"Dad, remember those old climbing pictures you had hanging on your walls down at your old law office? Of you out on the Nisqually Glacier in the '20s and '30s? Well, I once asked you why there was a loop tied to the climbing rope about a body-length from where you were tied in with a French bowline. You said that in case of a fall, the shaft of the ice axe could be shoved through that

Figure 8 BFH, age 16, on Mount Rainier in the 1920s. He is roped up with a loop near his waist to allow for a static belay. If a rope team member falls, the shaft of the axe is driven down through the loop into the snow to stop the fall.

loop for an instant belay. I didn't have time to tie the knot when you fell, Dad, but I did manage to take a turn of the rope around the axe."

BFH chuckled again, adding a smile. "You saved my life."

"Yes, Dad, but I saved mine, too. Necessity is a mother." At that we continued our laugh.

"And the next stop would have been the oyster beds," BFH concluded.

My beloved gray Weimaraner, Schatze, died years ago, an old dog, at the end of a life well-lived. Yet I had a feeling she was there in the room with dad and me, reminiscing, comforting.

# 9   The Crampons

*"Crampons are the equivalent of a big belay."*
–Frank Maranville

Crampons are an essential element in a snow and ice climber's gear. My first pair were heavy old ten-points with wire bales at the heels and a welter of straps hanging off of them. But before crampons are discussed, perspective may be gained by describing what it is like to climb without them.

In 1960, I climbed Mount Saint Helens. I did it in late summer and without crampons. It was a crisp, windy day with good visibility. The glacier above the Dog's Head was hard snow and ice. I was short-roped to Frank Maranville, my dad's climbing companion-in-crime. Dad was on another rope with Jerry Shimek. As BFH used to say, "If you fall here, the next stop is the oyster beds." This was an appropriate observation, as the fall-line on Saint Helens is thirty-five to forty degrees, and extends, Mount Fuji-fashion, for three miles straight down. So a climber falling near the top will be moving at a blistering (and deadly), speed within two hundred feet in the conditions we experienced. Not that the situation was uncommon on Saint Helens. It was painfully common, since the bulk of the mountain was below nine thousand feet. That meant the snow would repeatedly freeze and thaw, consolidate, and turn to ice. Even water-ice, the kind skaters use on level rinks. I recall a later news story of a climbing team's fall: A climber was on the top of the Dog's Head when he saw a rope team slip near the false summit 2,500 feet above. By the time the three unfortunates rag-dolled past him, they were "thirty feet in the air and still roped together. They looked like a giant slinky." Welcome to the oyster beds.

My own first ascent of Saint Helens, though successful, was anxious. Without crampons, I had to seek out nubs of snow and ice to get a grip with my boots. Vibram soles, though wonderful new technology for the time, didn't stick well to ice. They still don't. My ropemate and mentor Maranville had crampons. Yet I could visualize slipping and pulling him off balance. Fortunately I tiptoed up without suffering the event. We climbed up through wind-fluted rime ice mantling the false summit and then staggered through ripping gusts of wind across the long open crater to the true summit.

## AVOIDING THE SUDDEN STOP

Maranville educated me on the summit walk: "You know, George, geologically, Saint Helens is a violent volcano."

Figure 9 Author on Saint Helens, 1960. The summit is in the background.

"Why?" I asked, between gusts.

"Because it erupted in the 1840s and is likely to erupt again soon." His words were prophetic. Mount Saint Helens would erupt explosively again exactly twenty years later, a mere geological nanosecond away; and the very glaciers and rocks we stood on would be gone–dispersed eastward over the rest of Washington, Idaho, Montana, and points east. But today the wind whipped his words, and my interest in them, away. I had my hands full just putting one foot in front of the other. Besides, the mountain was sparklingly beautiful. Spindrift, kicked up by the wind, swirled around us like diamonds in the harsh sunlight. They wiled in dazzling wisps around my feet, arms and head. I was ethereal.

BFH, Maranville, Shimek, and I signed the summit register, nested in the remains of an old fire lookout, ate our lunch, and then headed back down. Down went well. By early afternoon the snow softened and "plunged" nicely, except for several crevassed areas of water-ice, over which I carefully walked, with Maranville's encouragement. Back at the Dog's Head, Maranville took a photo of Shimek, BFH, and me. We were happy. We unroped and glissaded down from the Dog's Head and slogged back to the car. I was dead tired but thrilled at what I'd done.

Figure 10 Jerry Shimek, BFH, and the author on Saint Helens, 1960.

Climb forward a season to 1961. I was twelve and on my first ascent of Little Tahoma. We stopped at the edge of the Whitman Glacier, dug our crampons out of packs, spent endless minutes trying to untangle them, laid them out neatly on the snow, and stepped in. Putting on old-style crampons was always frustrating. Each crampon had to be perfectly flush with the snow or ground, with straps splayed out of the way. Each of the little steel rings that connected the straps to the body of the crampon had to be flipped to the outside, otherwise one could be happily threading the straps only to discover that the last ring wasn't turned out and was jammed under the boot. Of course this necessitated starting the donning process all over again by taking one's boot out, which jumbled the crampon. Again the toothy metal beast had to be carefully laid out, rings out. The metal bale on the crampon fit snuggly up over the heal welt of the climbing boot. If one neglected to do that, no matter how tightly the crampons were strapped on, they would work loose. And experiencing a loose crampon at the wrong time and place could have lethal consequences, which could include oyster beds and sudden stops. I was proud that I had put on my crampons with little hassle. Both BFH and Maranville double-checked them and nodded approval. Little did BFH know that I had practiced repeatedly at home on our kitchen floor.

"How did these puncture holes get on my floor?"

"Gee Mom, I don't know. Maybe it's time we cut the dog's nails."

Back at the notch on the Whitman Glacier I stamped my feet on the hard snow. For the first time they felt stable.

Maranville, gave me a pep talk: "Now, George, having crampons on your feet on snow and ice is the equivalent of being always on a big belay. Your feet will stick like glue in most conditions." Maranville was a chemist, so he could not help talking in chemical terms and adding that last caveat: "In most conditions."

Figure 11 Rappelling off a serac with new crampons.

"Be sure to walk wide. You don't want to hook your legs or pants with them."

"Makes good sense," I thought to myself.

Off we climbed in two teams of two—Maranville and me on one rope, and BFH and Jerry Shimek on the other. With each plant of the foot, and as the Whitman Glacier steepened into the upper reaches of Little Tahoma, I gained confidence. At the exit ramp onto the final rock pitches of the climb, we took off our crampons and left them at the edge of the snow. In the early 1960s it was common to do a whole climb without seeing another party, and so it was on this July day. We had the big mountain to ourselves.

"Maranville and I are going up a little ways to reconnoiter the route. You and Jerry stay here," BFH said.

Jerry and I leaned back and rested. The sun shown softly on two tired bodies, and in a blink we were both asleep. I dreamed that I was back at home laying in the green grass of my backyard with my dog Schatze. Her head was in my lap and I was petting her warm velvety ears.

"OK, we found the route." Maranville's words startled Jerry and me awake. I regretted being jerked out of my backyard, out of the pleasant green of the grass and trees, and back into this menacing vertical place, colored in blinding contrasts of dark and light.

Figure 12 Little Tahoma as seen from the Emmons Glacier, Mount Rainier.

We scrambled up the exit ramp, and climbed into a rock chimney that took us to the summit ridge. The ridge was the scariest, airiest place I'd ever been. To the right the north face plunged thousands of feet down to the Emmons Glacier. The drop on the left hand was a little kinder, but as we worked our way along to the summit, it steepened into its own sheer drop down the south side to the Ingraham Glacier. The summit spire, or "plug," appeared to be balanced precariously in thin air, ready to topple over at any time. Behind the spire to the west loomed the massive white bulk of Mount Rainier, separated from Little Tahoma by crow's flight mile.

"OK, Frank, I've got you on belay, go ahead." BFH had set up a sitting belay by a large rock outcrop. Maranville eased across to the summit rock. I had expected him to climb an interior chimney, the obvious route up the spire, but he didn't. Instead he deftly tiptoed to the right out onto the sheer north face, and calmly climbed it the last few feet to the top. Jerry and I looked at each other.

"No way I'm going up like that," Jerry said.

Maranville sat down, flipped the rope around his body in a belay, and said, "Belay on," indicating it was time for us to climb. The rope to the summit was now belayed at both ends.

"All right, Jerry, clip your carabiner into the rope between Maranville and me and go," BFH directed. I watched as Jerry dropped down into the notch separating the ridge from the summit spire. Below him the rock dropped steeply a few feet, then disappeared into air. Jerry methodically negotiated the pitch.

"How many can you accommodate up there?" dad asked Maranville.

"Only Jerry and me," he said.

"OK, we'll shuttle Jerry back and then send George over."

"Dad, I don't want to go."

"Well you're going," BFH said. "Next fall you'll be in school telling everyone that you climbed Little Tahoma, and I'm not going to make a liar out of you."

Jerry climbed back, unclipped, and sat down behind BFH. "Its fine, Georgie, no sweat," he said, giving me a pat on the back. I clipped in and eased down into the notch. I realized that, though it looked impossible to this twelve year old, it wasn't. It was actually fun. I was on a solid fixed rope, the holds on the rock were numerous, and in no time I scrambled up next to Maranville.

Figure 13 On the summit ridge of Little Tahoma, 1960.

"Congratulations, George," he said. "The register's open there. Sign it just below where Jerry did." I signed my name proudly, looked around my aerie for a few minutes, then shuttled back down the rope to dad's position on the ridge. BFH then climbed to the top, signed the register, descended back to us and belayed Maranville, who came down last.

We then climbed back down to the top of the snow, and put on our crampons again for the trek down the glacier. As temper-testing as it was to put on crampons, I must say that they revolutionized snow and ice climbing. I loved them for that "big belay" they provided. The crampons worked as well downhill as they had uphill. The snow was perfect for them, and as I walked down the steep upper Whitman confidence grew. A couple hours later I took off my new crampons with the rest of the party, and slogged back to our camp at Summerland. Hikers were there now, enjoying the afternoon in the flowered meadow. As we packed up our gear and headed out, a hiker pointed to Jerry and me.

"Did you two little guys climb that?" he said incredulously, pointing to the top of Little Tahoma.

"Yup," Jerry replied.

"I can't believe it."

"Well, all you have to do is climb up there and check the register," Jerry said. "The name is Shimek." The hiker didn't answer.

Cramponing up Mount Rainier with guided clients was another matter entirely. Most had never climbed before, let alone tested their feet on a big glaciated mountain like Rainier. Therefore, we required them to keep their crampons on from the time they left Camp

## AVOIDING THE SUDDEN STOP

Muir until they arrived back there after the technical parts of the trip were completed. This was because putting on those old-style crampons consumed too much time. In the wee hours, just before roping up, we would assist clients in putting on their crampons, making sure they were properly attached to boots and fit snugly. Even though the standard guided routes were mostly over glaciers, there are also significant portions of the trail that led through rock and scree. We constantly checked the clients' feet, looking for rocks that might have been stuck in between the crampon points and could subsequently cause an ankle roll, a sprain, or even a fall. In all my climbs with the guide service, I cannot recall completing one without fixing malfunctions with clients' crampons. Usually they merely worked loose, but sometimes the whole crampon would come off of a boot. Murphy's Law dictated that it would always happen in the worst possible spot, on a steep icy slope or directly under objective hazards such as ice or rockfall areas. Fortunately, in my experience, and in those of my clients, sudden stops or other equally untoward fates were avoided. The Gibraltar route was notorious for rock-in-crampon incidents. Legendary climbing ranger Bill Butler broke his ankle by catching a stone in his crampon just below the Beehive, circa 1964.

Wind gusts and fatigue factored into a client phenomenon the guides termed a "flapper." A flapper was when some hapless client, perhaps staggering on rubbery legs, or buffeted by the wind, or both, would catch the inseam of his trouser leg with his inner crampon points. The result was often a sizable tear along the inseam, thus resulting in a flapper.

"Hey Gary, look back at your fifth client," I might yell up.

Gary Ullin would look back to see a pant leg streaming sideways in the wind.

"Okay, George. I'll stop. Come on up and fix it."

As I was climbing to the hapless client, I would yank off a glove, reach into a pocket of my parka, and pull out a curved needle. It was prethreaded with about two feet of dental floss. Dental floss was perfect for quick mending, being strong and weatherproof. I'd reach out, grab the flapper, pull it back around the victim's leg, and quickly stitch up the tear, which by now extended to the crotch. As I looped upward through the material, I enjoyed saying, "Now we are beginning to get close to sensitive areas so it would behoove you to remain very still." This was one of the few times when I never had the slightest problem with client noncompliance.

The scuffling of crampons over rocks in the darkness was a sound and light show. Flinty sparks could be seen accompanying clanking metal. The metal spikes rang like wind chimes out of tune.

Modern crampons are now of the more rigid and step-in design. They are vastly easier to put on, sport only one strap, and have no flopping metal rings at the anchor points. With the passing of the 1960s, so passed floppy rings and straps and all of the colorful frustrations that went with them. In my later days of guiding, I built my own pair of step-in crampons fashioned from an old pair of ski bindings. They snapped on neatly around the grooved heel welts of my Lowe Nanga Parbat high-altitude boots. I took a pair of twelve-point Grivels, cut the binding rings off at the front ends, and installed a metal cross piece that fit over the welt of the boot's toe. As I now had both ends of the crampons tightened when I snapped in the spring binding, all I needed was a security strap to prevent the rear binding from unsnapping, and one through the midrings to hold the crampon against the sole of the boot. This system was fast and effective.

At the end of every guiding season, my dad would meticulously resharpen the now-dulled points of my Grivels. By my third and last year at the guide service, my crampon points were half the length they were when new. But I preferred the shorter points. They didn't ball up snow under my feet as much and were more comfortable. Speaking of comfort, the best crampons on that score were a set of chromoly steel ten-point slants that a client donated to me after a climb. Chromoly crampons were just out on the market then. They were light, strong, and the slant of the front two points significantly diminished the resistance of driving one's toes into the snow or ice hour after hour.

One hot early August day in 1966, Gary Ullin and I were guiding a party down off of the Ingraham headwall following a successful summit. It was about two in the afternoon, and we passed a group of four Mexicans. They were wandering up the route, roped together with clothesline about fifteen feet apart. They carried ice axes and were using crampons, so they got that right. However, as we moved closer, we realized that their crampons were tied on over open sandals. Ullin tried to talk them into turning back, but they claimed not to understand and kept on going. To this day I have no idea whether that crampon and sandals group, roped together with clothesline, ever made it to the summit. I surmise they did, because it is my experience and belief that special angels often watch over innocent and clueless climbers. Back at Camp Muir we discovered that these fellows had tossed our gear out of the bunks and placed their own in them. It was no big deal, because we were merely packing up and slogging back down to Paradise anyway.

The Mountain beckons those from all walks.

# 10 The Avalanche

*"It was a good drill."* –BFH

My father, BFH, considered Mount Washington to be an excellent "shake-down" climb for the new season. Situated near our town of Shelton, Washington, on the Olympic Peninsula, it was also only a short drive from home.

It was an early May day. A storm had passed through the day before, dumping snow in the mountains, but today was foggy and calm. Fog was a common companion on northwest climbs, but particularly in the Olympics, which squeeze moisture from the Pacific Ocean that surrounds them.

On this day the party was repeating the eastern couloir route I'd done the year before. We were a small group, both in numbers and strength. BFH and Frank

Maranville led the group as usual. Jack Jeffery, Stan Parker, Jerry Shimek, and I comprised the balance. Jack was the father of Bob Jeffery, the climber who fell into the crevasse on Little Tahoma's Frying Pan Glacier three years later and nearly carried my sister with him (see "The Knot").

Our party hiked to the end of the approach trail, traversed left around rock outcrops, and entered the first couloir. We roped up. BFH, Shimek, and Stan Parker were on one. Frank Maranville, Jack Jeffery, and I were on the other. In the couloir we stood in knee-deep new snow. The fog was lifting and the temperature was rising. As we broke a tedious trail upward, we noticed snow beginning to peel off and slide down through the little side gullies funneling into our path. We were entering avalanche country. In another hour, we climbed out of the first couloir into the large snow bowl that reposes midway up Washington's eastern face.

Figure 14 Taken just before starting up the avalanche chute.

During a rest stop, BFH and Maranville conferred. "What do you think, Frank?" Maranville, who had been slathering himself with clown-white sunscreen as the sun broke through, looked around. Where we stood in the bowl, the new snow in many of the side gullies was breaking free and spilling all around us.

"It's not looking good," Maranville responded in his usual understated way. "Should we bag the climb?"

BFH glanced around, thinking. "No. If we try to go down the couloir we just climbed and are hit by an avalanche, it's the oyster beds. There is no run-out below it, and we'll be washed over the cliff at the bottom. Here, even though the couloir above us hasn't peeled off yet, at least if it does we'll have a run-out here in the bowl. We can't go back. We have to summit and return by the standard route, which is less exposed in these conditions."

Maranville pondered a moment and nodded. We were going up the unstable second couloir. It thrust itself at forty-five degrees half a mile up through towering rock buttresses, where it terminated at an exit ramp just below the summit. Maranville led off, I was tied into the middle, and Jack Jeffery brought up the rear of our rope. BFH followed with Jerry Shimek and Stan Parker on his rope. We were making good time notwithstanding the soft snow. The bowl began to shrink below us.

"Avalanche!" someone yelled. I looked up. Roiling toward us and gaining speed and volume with every foot surged a wall of wet, hissing snow. Maranville turned his head back toward me.

"George, it's OK, it's not a big one. Dig your ice axe in and hold on."

I saw him do the same, ramming the shaft of his axe into the snow. The forward wall of the avalanche hit him like an explosion. My view shifted to slow motion as I watched Maranville's red Cruiser pack coming straight at me, rotating lazily until the legs under the pack were where the head should be. Then I was hit.

The world went white. I was plunging downward and violently rolled as if in a giant washing machine. My rope was pulling me under. I fought against it, trying to swim upward to the top, but "up" kept changing as I continued to tumble. I noticed that the shaft and point of my ice axe, which was attached to my wrist, was aimed straight at my stomach. I was turning slowly over it, the relative position between my body and the shaft of the axe remaining fixed and unchanged. I tried to brush it away with my right arm, but it was no use. Snow alternated with sky as the avalanche, now an enveloping giant, spun me down hundreds of feet into the bowl below. So this is what it's like to die, I thought. The frank detachment of the thought interested me. It was flat, direct, and simple. It supplanted fear. Then I felt myself slowing down. Snow was compacting tightly around me like wet cement. It became dead quiet.

"George, are you all right? Where are you?" I turned toward Maranville's voice. He was sitting on top of jumbled snow only feet away. His hooded green windbreaker was darkly water-stained. His red Cruiser pack lay next to him. I looked at his face. He had a faint smile, but I noticed that snow was packed between his clown-white face and his dark glasses. He looked like Dr. Strangelove's ghost.

"I'm right in front of you," I said, my voice quavering, "And no I'm not all right. I am trapped from the waist down and can't move my legs!"

Maranville and Jack Jeffery gathered themselves, walked over, and dug me out. I was able to stand up and take stock of myself. There were three puncture holes through my tight red wool ski sweater, put there by the point of my ice axe. Three times, as I fought to push the axe away during the avalanche, the whole point and shaft had plunged cleanly through the sides of my sweater. By some miracle I hadn't suffered a scratch. But it left me shaken. I took time to silently thank my shoulder angel.

Figure 15 Maranville and Jeffery digging me out of the avalanche

Maranville looked at the holes, patted me on the shoulder, and said, "George, that was close. We were lucky, but we have to climb back up."

"No! I'm not going back up there," I blurted.

"We have no choice. It hasn't yet avalanched in the couloir below us, so we can't go back down the route we just came up."

Figure 16 Parker and BFH awaiting our return up the avalanche chute.

"No way, I'm not going back up."

"Look, George, I understand how you feel. We have survived this avalanche unhurt. The chute above us has now been flushed out, so now when we climb up it, we won't have to worry about any more avalanches coming down there. Let's go."

I put my pack back on. My legs were shaking. A half mile up the couloir, BFH, Shimek, and Parker's rope team had been spared. They were just slightly to the right of the slide's path. I heard BFH's piercing two-finger whistle signaling us to get a move on. Back up the chute we climbed. All around us now, side gullies were dumping smaller avalanches into the snow bowl below us. The sun came out and heated up our surroundings. Everywhere I looked the steepening slopes seemed alive and moving. BFH and his team waited until our rope neared, then proceeded, kicking steps up the steep couloir. We had nearly made it up next to them when Maranville cried out, "Avalanche!"

I jerked my head up and, sure enough, around the corner above snaked another one. The sliding snow was not nearly as big this time, but it was evident, as it hissed toward us, that there was plenty of force behind it.

"Dig your shaft in and hang on as hard as you can!" This time Maranville had no encouraging words. Our team dug in and braced for impact. I glanced up to see snow boiling angrily around Maranville's legs. I put my head down and clung to my axe with all my strength. A small wall of snow hit, and for an instant I feared losing my grip. I prayed. But then I noticed that I'd held on long enough that I was now on an island, and the rest of the avalanche was splitting and spilling around both sides of me. I looked up to see BFH, Shimek, and Parker sliding toward me. They had not been able to hold against the second avalanche, but their ride was kinder than ours. It was more like a sitting glissade. As BFH slid past, taking his turn to ride into the snow bowl, he looked over and said, "Don't worry."

"I won't," I said.

I was frustrated, angry, and afraid. Mount Washington seemed determined to kill us that day—me in particular. My mentor, Frank Maranville, had lied to me when he'd said the first avalanche was "not a big one." He had lied again when he told me that returning up this now "flushed out" couloir would be safe and that there would be no more avalanches. The climb so far had been near fatal. That was my stark young view of it. And the climb was not over.

Our team waited on the scoured snow. The couloir was at its steepest here, over forty-five degrees. I watched as BFH and the other two black dots down in the bowl gathered themselves up and slowly slogged back toward us.

We summited Mount Washington on that trying, and nearly dying, day back in May of 1961. We descended by the standard route and walked away from the mountain. I avoided the sudden stop...and the oyster beds.

The subject of the avalanche came up again as Dad lay dying with cancer. He no longer tried to make light of the event.

"That was grim," I said. "I was sure I was going to die."

"It was at least a thousand tons," he said.

"Plenty to kill the whole lot of us," said I.

"Yes," BFH nodded. He had a tired wry smile. "But it just wasn't the day for that to happen."

## AVOIDING THE SUDDEN STOP

"The day is there for us all. That's our mortal lot. But I'm sure glad I made it past twelve years old," I said.

"I'm glad you did too, George. And yes, the day is there."

The afternoon sun shone through the bedroom window on the foot of BFH's bed. The shadow-limbs of the fir trees outside furrowed the light. Dad was home. I was with him. Our voices fell silent a moment.

"I'm proud of you Dad," I said.

"I'm proud of you too, George," he said.

The Old Man of the Mountain was sleepy. He drifted off. I let him.

## 11  Eat Cold, Drink Hot

*"Less mess, less fuel, less time."* –BFH

My father's perils with his 1920s-built Primus stove forced him to reconsider rituals of high camp eating. BFH ultimately hit upon the formula: eat cold, drink hot. The premise was simple. We were up there to climb, not eat. Therefore, for the two or three days required of a normal Northwest mountaineering exercise, one could easily forego eating hot meals. BFH thus pre-prepared main courses, if they could be called that. All meat was steak, which he precooked to well done, and which had a shelf life of a couple of days, even in the heat. It was heavily garnished with salt and pepper, and then placed in rubber-banded aluminum tins, which he labeled "Steak." There is a story behind this.

"Dad, can we eat the steak sandwiches tonight?" I

asked on the first day of the climb.

"No, eat your peanut butter sandwiches. I'm saving the steak for tomorrow."

It was a warm night and hot subsequent day's trip up Little Tahoma. At ten o'clock, on a rest stop on the Whitman Glacier, BFH finally gave the green light: "OK, we can eat our steak sandwiches now." I opened mine up, didn't like what I smelled, and opted out. BFH ate his, and within a half hour was throwing up. BFH summited Little Tahoma with food poisoning, demonstrating his usual iron resolve. From then on, all meat was cooked well, sans bread and mayo, and packed in its own tins.

That took care of the entree. Side cuisine consisted of Sailor Boy Pilot Bread, which was a large round flat hardtack, topped with a slab of cheese, followed by raisin or oatmeal cookies, and dried fruits such as apricots. Meanwhile, BFH would coax a few liters of hot water out of his stove. Into our steaming tin cups would go a bullion cube, or a teabag, or tea with a lemon drop.

Pre-climb breakfast did not include starting the stove at all. We merely had a swig of cold water and oatmeal-raisin cookies. Lunches were composed of Sailor Boy Pilot Bread topped with a slab of cheese, topped in turn with a slice of Hickory Farm summer sausage. The Sailor Boy hardtack thus functioned as an edible plate. Stops where snacks could be accessed consisted of GORP (Good Old Raisins and Peanuts) trail mix, a slice of summer sausage, and water.

## AVOIDING THE SUDDEN STOP

There was one eating scheme with which BFH experimented that did not work out well, however. Tom Needham, our Shelton neighbor and climbing colleague, took the mantra a step further—"Eat and Drink Cold." This was done by simply carrying cans of Nestlé's Nutrament chocolate protein shakes instead of regular food. In theory it was brilliant. BFH seized the concept, went down to the local pharmacy, which was the only place it was sold, and bought out the entire supply, to Needham's chagrin. Little Tahoma, 1963, was again the testbed. Needham and I processed the shakes well enough. BFH did not. The Nutrament plugged him up. Completely constipated, by the time we hiked out to the trailhead he was walking wide. The Nutrament food experiment thus met a hemorrhoidal end.

BFH went back to the old formula. It may not have been the best or preferred provender, but it worked well. It was efficient, did not rely on much hot water, cut down on carrying cooking utensils and pots, and was fast. Fast was good for BFH. He wanted to clear camp and get on with the climb as soon as possible. And since we never used tents, and chose to bivouac instead, this eating process dovetailed nicely.

We ate to climb.

## 12 The Curse of the Stove

*"Fire in the hole!"*

It was a curse. It was as if we began every climb from below sea level. With "The Stove," all trips started in Death Valley.

The Stove was an old Primus, manufactured in Sweden sometime in the 1920s, which was when the young BFH had bought it. In its time I'm sure it was state of the art for mountaineering. It came in a red-and-gold tin box five inches square and five inches deep.

All parts of it were brass and fit snug in their places. On the inside of the lid BFH had written: "Seven-eighths kerosene, one-eighth white gas." This cryptic phrase was both a clue and an admission. It signified the Stove's extreme sensitivity to fuel mixtures and the time and trouble it took to arrive at its optimum. Its optimum was when it actually worked for more than fifteen minutes.

For BFH, it was not enough that he subjected himself and others to storms, wind, cold, bivouacs without tents, altitude, sunburn, and rock and ice fall. He had to bring the Stove.

Figure 17 The Stove.

Ritual always accompanied its setup. BFH would lay out a small piece of rolled plastic mat. I'd call it the prayer rug, because BFH spent so much time kneeling over it. The Stove was placed on top and its box opened. First, out came the brass fuel tank that was the contraption's base. Then came the throat, or fuel ignition chamber. It was screwed onto the fuel tank. Next came the metal arms with a bracket for the burner plate. The arms splayed wide at their tops and also functioned as the platform for the cook pot. Then came the doughnut shaped lighting ring, and small burner plate, which were placed over the tiny hole in the center of the ignition chamber whence flame was to come. The Stove now stood proud and complete. Directions to it were useless because they were in Swedish. BFH carried them in the box anyway, perhaps hoping we'd someday find a Swedish stove-fixer on the mountain with us.

BFH would then pressurize the fuel tank with a small pump on its side, pour a few drops of white gas on the lighting ring, turn a tiny valve on the ignition chamber until he heard a hissing or sputtering, then strike a match. A whoosh of flame would shoot up, and BFH would scramble to adjust it with the valve, but usually he caused the fire to go out. It was relit and would go out. BFH, now frustrated and usually swearing, would crank the valve open on the third try. The third try was the most exciting. He'd touch it off and fire would roar three feet in the air, blowing off the burner plate. By now the ignition chamber had heated enough to allow the Stove to settle down into its sputtering, chugging routine. Snow would be placed in the cook pot for melting. A few minutes later, the sputtering and chugging would worsen. The blue cooking flame would turn yellow and whoosh up again, leaving the aluminum cook pot coated in fine black soot. More swearing. Out would come the tiny reamer. BFH would meticulously clean out the little hole, and the process would start over: pump ten times; prime with white gas; turn the valve; light the stove; swear; fiddle with the valve until the flame again turned blue; swear; and put the pot back on. Nothing embodied a greater frustration, failure, and famine than the Stove. At least it was consistent.

In 1964, on a climb up the Emmons Glacier, BFH finally left the Stove at home and brought along a new Bluet stove with several butane canisters. But the curse followed him.

We were camped on the glacier above Steamboat Prow next to a big crevasse. Our dinner fare also included something new: freeze-dried food. We melted snow for the climb and boiled water in the dinner pot, but just as BFH was preparing to heat up the entree of beef stew, which now took its turn in the pot, the Bluet's fuel canister went dry. He inserted a full one, but somehow did not seat it properly with the stove. This caused a leak. When BFH lit the match, the stove erupted in a fireball. Swearing, he drop-kicked the burning Bluet into an adjacent crevasse, which lit up an impressive blue. Maybe that's how the stove got its name.

"Hey, Dad," I said. "We have this pot of freeze-dried beef stew. It's in warm water, but it's definitely not cooked. What should we do?"

"We have a hot stove over here, and it's not being used," Maranville offered.

"We're fine," dad said.

"One mouthful takes forever to chew up," Catherine said.

Tom Needham and I started giggling.

"A one bite dinner," I said in a low voice to Tom, out of dad's earshot.

"Yeah," he chuckled, "it's like that Brylcreme commercial." Then he sang the TV jingle: "Brylcreem—A Little Dab'll Do Ya, Brylcreem—You'll look so debonaire. Brylcreem—The gals'll all pursue ya; Simply put a little on your hair." We laughed.

"What's so humorous over there?" BFH asked over his chew.

"Nothing, Dad," I said. "We were just laughing about your formerly new stove. Do you think we will have to go back to using the old Primus?"

"I don't know what the hell I'm going to do about it," he retorted. "You two clowns get your sleeping bags unrolled."

On the next day's summit climb, all of us who'd eaten the uncooked stew—BFH, Catherine, Tom Needham, and I—suffered terrible, unrelenting gas. It got worse as we gained altitude, but not just for us; Maranville and the rest of the party following us suffered mightily as well. The Mountain that morning didn't provide enough wind to blow ours away.

BFH gave me the Stove just before he died in 2008. I had no idea that he'd kept it. If any piece of equipment deserved an ignominious end it was the Stove. He also gave me his old climbing clothing. Neatly folded and rubber-banded in a plastic sack was BFH's orange felt hunter's hat that he used on hot climbing days. It had black soot smudges all around the brim. I immediately recognized what had caused them. They were the lasting legacy of the Stove.

## 13 THE EPIC

*"An ordinary climb rendered difficult by a dangerous combination of weather, injuries, darkness, lack of preparedness or other adverse factors." –Glossary of Climbing Terms, Wikipedia*

It was 1961, and I was twelve years old. By then I had summited many peaks in the Northwest Cascades, including Mount Adams, Mount Saint Helens, and Little Tahoma. BFH decided to take a run at Mount Shuksan in the North Cascades. I was a competent climber, but hadn't yet gained the strength and endurance that would come with growing into adolescence.

The climb began auspiciously enough. Five of us from Shelton made up our party: BFH, Frank Maranville, Don Jackson, Dave Banning, and me. After a long drive from Shelton up to the Mount Baker Lodge, we donned our gear and hiked the trail into Lake Ann, the start of the Fisher Chimneys route on Mount Shuksan. For the first time we carried a small transistor radio. After we'd set up camp and cooked dinner, BFH and Maranville huddled over the radio listening to a scratchy weather forecast from KOMO in Seattle.

"The weather's changing," BFH said. "A storm front is moving in and expected to hit in about twelve hours. What do you think Frank?"

"It's not favorable," Maranville replied. "I suppose we can camp here tonight, pull up stakes in the morning, and go home." He paused. "But we've come a long way from Shelton just to do that." Such words beget epics. They both thought for a moment.

"What if," Maranville said, "instead of sleeping here tonight, we do the climb when we finish with dinner? We could summit and descend back to camp before the bad weather hits."

"I was thinking the same thing," said BFH. "OK, let's give it a go." And that was it. We were taking a shot literally in the dark. Neither BFH nor Maranville had been on Mount Shuksan before. Neither knew the Fisher Chimneys route.

We readied our climbing packs and stowed sleeping and cooking gear under tarps. BFH and I each carried Sears hunters' headlamps, powered by large six-volt dry cells. Maranville, Jackson, and Banning carried weaker headlamps or flashlights. We started the climb around six that evening, walking the path over sloping meadows to the Fisher Chimneys. We roped up: Maranville and I on the lead team, and BFH, Banning, and Jackson following.

The chimneys were a labyrinth of gullies interspersed with steep rock steps. It was landscape perfect for luring a party off route. It did. Daylight faded and we switched on our lights. Several times Maranville made a wrong turn up a gully and had to return. The key was to locate white arrows painted on the rocks to stay on the route, but these were faded and easily missed. We missed several and had to backtrack.

"Rock!" Maranville shouted back. We hunkered down and ducked. As we moved haltingly along, it seemed that every rope length we were either dislodging rocks on each other or dodging them from the darkness above. It was not just nerve-wracking, it was chronically exposed and dangerous. Several times, just as BFH and Maranville were considering scrubbing the climb, we'd locate a faded arrow on a rock and decide to continue. Time ticked by. Finally, at about ten o'clock, we exited Fisher Chimneys on Shuksan Arm and put on crampons on the snow below Winnie Slide. Maranville and I climbed toward the slide. On the right hand, a big waterfall was tumbling off toward the Lower Curtis Glacier. Over its rumbling we heard shouts from below. It was BFH.

"Banning, get moving. No, we're not going back. Get up and walk!"

Maranville coiled me in. "I think Banning's in trouble. He's freezing up."

"What do you mean?" I asked.

"I think he's got acrophobia. That's where someone's fear of heights takes over, petrifies them, and they can't move."

"It that serious?"

"Yes," Maranville said. His voice was flatly analytical. "Not only for Banning, but also for the rest of us."

Why we didn't turn around right then is beyond me. But we didn't. With the surfacing of Dave's acrophobia, the pace of the climb dropped further. More time slipped by. BFH continued leaning on Dave to get him to move. The darkness, the yelling, both of encouragement and orders to "Move!" turned the climb into a nightmare. And then the weather hit.

We had topped Winnie Slide, cut back across the Upper Curtis Glacier, and had started up the steep slopes of Hell's Highway toward the Sulfide Glacier. At five o'clock in the morning, the storm broke over us. It was as though it tried to shut out the daylight. My headlamp was still on, but BFH told me to turn it off. "We may need if for the way down," he said. An hour later found us finally on the Sulfide Glacier, climbing slowly toward Shuksan's summit pyramid. Dave was heroically trying to comply with BFH and Maranville's prodding. He fought the fear. At eight in the morning, the party gained the pyramid rocks. We took off our crampons.

"Don, you stay here with Dave. Get into the cleft of

this rock out of the wind and stay together for warmth. Maranville, George, and I will make a quick try at the top. OK?"

They nodded. I wish I could have stayed with them. The cold was creeping into my hands and feet. But off we climbed, in a storm building to a rage, and having just split the party. Maranville found a length of fixed rope. We hauled ourselves up and climbed another three hundred feet.

"Frank, the summit has to be close. The altimeter is showing nine thousand fifty feet."

"But now we have another problem," Maranville replied. "I can't see."

"What do you mean?"

"My glasses have iced up." Maranville was nearsighted and effectively blind without them. BFH paused.

"Dad, this is crazy. Let's go down. My hands and feet are freezing."

"All right, that's it. Let's pull the pin and get out of here."

With a blizzard howling, our team inched down off the summit pyramid. Maranville couldn't see his own feet. BFH had to reach up, grab Maranville's boots, and place them into holds. Finally reunited with Jackson and Banning, we fumbled to strap on our crampons.

"Dad, I can't feel to put on my crampons." I started crying. The emptiness of stress, cold, tiredness, and frustration swept over me. BFH came over and strapped them on. He put his arm around my shoulder.

"Hang in there son. I'm proud of you." With that he put on his pack and we headed down. His words of praise were so rare that I was immediately calmed. The misery and cold didn't matter as much.

Snow and fog were kiting across the Sulfide Glacier as the party started back. As we climbed down, my feet and hands began to thaw, and the pain was excruciating. At Hell's Highway, and again on Winnie Slide, both of our teams had to arrest falls. We were now running on more than thirty hours without sleep. Banning, though fearful, was now moving steadily, however. Jackson was leading, but he was so tired that he began to nod off in stride. He would fall, and Dave and BFH would arrest him and wake him up. Now BFH had to yell at Don to keep him awake.

As the party descended into the Fisher Chimneys, the blizzard stopped and was replaced by fog. The route traversed rock steps and gullies. Though no longer icy, they were wet and slick. BFH decided to reverse his rope. He would take the lead and route-find. Banning was following BFH in the middle, and Jackson now anchored the team. As I led down the last rope with Maranville bringing up the rear, I had just climbed off a steep rock step and was edging around a small corner into the next gully when I heard rock falling and muffled voices ahead. I rounded the corner and looked into the gully. Jackson was eighty feet down below Banning and BFH. Scraped and muddy, he groggily climbed back up.

"What happened?" I yelled.

## AVOIDING THE SUDDEN STOP

"Jackson fell, and Banning stopped him," BFH said.

Don had taken a leader fall in the gully and bounced eighty feet toward the cliffs that dumped into the Lower Curtis Glacier. Dave heard Don fall, turned around, and flipped the rope over a big rock outcrop. This belay saved the team. BFH was in a precarious traverse, and so was Banning, and Jackson had picked up enough speed to pull them all off. Banning, who had been consumed with acrophobia a few hours before, had instantly made the perfect decision to loop the rope over the outcrop. Jackson was jerked to a sudden stop. It woke him up.

"Don, what happened?" BFH asked, as he helped pull Jackson back up to the trail.

"I fell asleep," Don said. That likely saved him from injury. When he fell he was completely relaxed.

We stepped off the chimneys and into our camp at Lake Ann as the weather cleared. The sun came out. I was completely spent. Every judgment that day by both BFH and Maranville had been wrong. Turn-around decisions were presented at Lake Ann the day before, but they decided to "beat the storm." They lost too much time route-finding in the chimneys, but they pressed on, knowing a storm was imminent. They continued the climb when presented with a party member with acrophobia. They continued the climb knowing they had kids with them who were young and hadn't been able to sleep or rest. They continued to climb into the teeth of the storm, on a route and big mountain they did not know, despite knowing their party's deficits and deteriorating strengths. They split a weakened party under adverse conditions. But it was not over.

BFH and Maranville decided not to rest, but to break camp and hike out. On the long walk, with a heavy pack, I had a sense of being disembodied. I saw my feet moving but felt no connection to them. BFH had to hold on to my arm to assist me over the last ridge to the car. There dad decided to bite into a piece of hard candy. It broke his tooth.

Maranville had his Rambler wagon, but he intended to stop for the night in Bellingham to see Evelyn, his wife, who was taking college summer courses there. So the rest of us piled into BFH's 1958 Chrysler. Into the evening, BFH drove I-5 toward home. Finally, in Tacoma, he could drive no more.

"Jackson, are you OK to drive?" Don started out of a deep sleep.

"Yes," he replied.

BFH collapsed into the back seat and went to sleep immediately. Jackson was not far behind him.

I awoke to grinding metal. Our '58 Chrysler had crashed into the center guardrail near Fort Lewis. He had fallen asleep again. Don was able to limp the vehicle to the next off-ramp and pull in to a gas station. No one was hurt, but the Chrysler was totaled. From a phone booth, dad called mom and Catherine, who were vacationing in Sun Valley Idaho, to tell them what happened. They packed up immediately and headed home.

Don Jackson called his parents who drove up from Shelton and finally ferried us back home.

It was three o'clock the next morning when I crawled into bed. I slept twenty-six hours. For days afterward I jumped out of bed when I saw falling rocks coming at me in my dreams.

Though Mount Shuksan in 1961 was a fiasco, and a nightmare for this twelve-year-old, better judgment came of it. We walked away. BFH and Maranville never repeated their mistakes. Don Jackson and Dave Banning never climbed again. Dave went on to survive two tours with the US Army in Vietnam and to distinguish himself as a Cobra gunship pilot. He later told me that he did it partly to test the acrophobia that was triggered on Shuksan. It obviously was not a problem in that deadly combat environment. "I found that I had no fear of heights at all when I was enclosed by an airframe and canopy," he said.

If an epic trip in the mountains doesn't end lives, it changes them. It revives respect.

My epic Mount Shuksan adventure did not end with my return to the house in Shelton. When mom came home the whole nightmare had to be re-lived and critiqued. Dad and mom fought almost continually for the next week. It wore on my sister Catherine's nerves and on mine. We solved that by doing the usual family thing—we fought with each other. Sometimes, I thought, even Mount Shuksan seemed preferable.

BFH and I discussed the Shuksan fiasco during the

quiet moments of his last days. A wise-cracker to the end, dad summed up the experience as he slumped weakly in his favorite living room chair by the warmth of the gas-fired fireplace: "Yes, it all went to hell on that trip," he mused. "The weather went bad, we couldn't find the route, rockfall bombarded us, Banning had acrophobia, Jackson fell asleep every ten feet, Maranville couldn't see, you froze your hands, Jackson fell in the Chimneys, I broke my tooth, we totaled the car, and my wife came home."

BFH may have been a tough old bird losing his feathers, but he remained pithy.

## 14  THE HEADWALL

*A headwall is a good place to learn advanced climbing skills. But lessons can be hit or miss.*

I first climbed Mount Rainier in 1962, when I was thirteen years old. BFH was leading a party of a dozen or so, along with Frank Maranville, my older sister Catherine, and other climbing companions hailing from our hometown of Shelton, Washington. The weather was balmy that summer day in late July. We rolled our sleeping bags out on the flat roof of the public hut at Camp Muir and slept under the stars. At around one o'clock the next morning, we roped up and headed out across the Cowlitz Glacier. We made good time up through Cathedral Gap and out onto the Ingraham Flats. The stiletto profile of Little Tahoma stood sentry just to the east. It looked near enough to touch. Off to our left, the trail angled along the Ingraham toward Cathedral Rocks.

BFH tried to find a middling route through the crevasses, but he was forced ever farther to the left. We took a break at Cadaver Gap and then continued. The huge bulk of Gibraltar was now soaring hundreds of feet above us—directly above us. As I played my headlamp along its cliffs, the light caught reflections of huge icicles. They were as large as upended shipping containers, and they hung sullenly off of broken basalt ledges.

"Let's get a move on through this," BFH yelled out. "We don't want to be exposed here any longer than we have to be."

We stepped gingerly around chunks of ice and rocks that were now pockmarking our way. In climbing slang it was a "bowling alley." The falling rocks were the bowling balls and we were the pins. Quickly now, I said to myself. Another hundred feet up, I could see that the trail angled around a crevasse to the right and out of danger. Just a few more feet.

A thunderous crash broke the silence. I looked up to see chunks of ice and rock tumbling down on us. The rocks were splashing the snow in all directions as they hit and rolled through our party. I was the middle man on a three-man rope. Luckily we all sprinted in the same direction, and though debris bounded around and between us, no one was hit. Finally we stopped, panting, and looked back.

BFH, whose team was ahead of ours, called back,

## AVOIDING THE SUDDEN STOP

"Was anyone hit?"

Our team called back, "No," but further down the line Frank Maranville's voice was heard out of the darkness: "Yes. Stan's been hit, I think in the chest. But he can still walk."

"OK, let's get him up here where it's safe to take a look at him."

Stan Parker was stunned but able to walk his way up to us along with Maranville, my sister Catherine, and the rest of the party.

"Stan, what happened?" BFH asked.

"I tried to run from this big boulder that hit the snow just above me," Stan gasped. "But the front guy on my rope ran one way and the end guy ran in the opposite direction. I was trapped in the middle and couldn't move."

BFH put a consoling hand on Stan's shoulder. "Sorry. Where are you hurt? Is your head OK?"

"Yeah, my head's fine, but the rock hit the snow then bounced into my chest and knocked me over."

"Can you breathe?"

"Yes, but its real painful here on my left side," Stan said, pointing to his rib cage and wincing.

"How big was the rock?" BFH asked.

"About the size of a basketball."

Frank Maranville and BFH agreed that Stan should immediately head down. The question was whether to turn the whole party around.

Maranville answered that one without hesitation:

"I'll take Stan down to Muir. If he's stable, we'll wait there for you. If not, I'll get him down to the doctor at Paradise."

"You sure?" BFH asked. "We can turn this whole rodeo around right here."

"No," Maranville insisted, "we have a good day, and it's still early. You take the rest of the party and go for it."

Go for it we did. The incident must have cranked up everyone's adrenaline because BFH and our now-reduced party took off up the Ingraham headwall like it wasn't there. True to its name, the headwall is a fifty-degree ice slope about two rope lengths long that is formed as the Ingraham Glacier breaks southeast around the top of Gibraltar at 12,300 feet. The route from there to the top was straightforward. Notwithstanding rockfall and Stan Parker's mishap, we summited two hours faster than expected. BFH was concerned and wanted to get back down to check on Parker and Maranville, so we signed the summit register, had a drink of water and a bite to eat, and headed down.

Back at the headwall, I had my first exercise in crab-walking down steep ice. BFH was down below tutoring me.

"George, take your free hand and grab about halfway down the shaft of your ice axe. Keep your axe hand over the head just like you've been doing, so if you slip you can self-arrest. Now bend your knees; keep your boots and crampons pointing down the hill and flush with the slope. That's it. Now using your axe cross-body, put a little weight on the shaft as a solid third point of balance, but make sure you keep as much weight as possible out over your feet, like when you're skiing."

I eased myself down, feeling anything but stable.

"Don't edge your boots or heels into the hill. Place your feet firmly straight down and let the crampon take the weight. One small step at a time."

I slapped each crampon into the ice, taking tiny steps. Thigh muscles burned. About midway down the headwall, and in the steepest spot, my crampons started to skid out from under me, but, counter-intuitively, I shifted more weight downhill and the skidding stopped.

"Good!" BFH exclaimed. "You've got it nailed now, son." BFH was not an exclaimer. My climbing confidence took a soaring leap that day on the Ingraham Headwall.

The rest of the descent, down past Cadaver Gap, the bowling alley under Gibraltar, the Ingraham Flats, through Cathedral Gap, and back across the Cowlitz Glacier to Camp Muir went swiftly and without incident. Frank Maranville was there with Stan Parker. Stan looked much better. He remained in pain, but aspirin made it manageable. X-rays later revealed that he had broken two ribs but sustained no other injuries. Stan had lucked out. Odds and luck are a fickle lot. They may favor or run out on you as they please.

I have one last impression of my first climb of Rainier: utter fatigue. When we finally arrived at the parking lot at Paradise, it was full of summer visitors of all ages, types, and sizes. BFH unlocked our white 1961 Plymouth station wagon, the dusty, wet, sweat-soaked gear was loaded, and Catherine and I collapsed into soft car seats.

"Here, hold these," BFH said. "I'm going to the ranger station to sign us out." I took the car keys and held them.

The pleasant summer breeze wafted around me, mingled with the conversations and laughter of passersby, the opening and closing of car doors, and engines idling. I nodded into a deep sleep. *Clank.* The sound of keys hitting the car floor woke me up. I looked down, picked them up, and held them in my hand. *Clank.* Again I startled awake, picked up the keys, and held them. *Clank.* This mindless motorized cycle repeated eight or ten times before BFH came back to the car.

"George, why didn't you just put the keys on the seat next to you?" He had noticed, with amusement, what was happening.

"Because you told me to hold on to them," I said as I again drifted off into an exhausted sleep.

Stan Parker never went on to summit Mount Rainier. Indeed, he called it good and ended his climbing career. It is understandable, because Stan learned an enduring lesson—that in the great bowling alley of life, fate sometimes picks up a spare.

# 15 Mount Adams Shuffleboard

*"Look at that baby go!"* –Tom Needham

The game's inception was on the north ridge of Mount Adams. The rules were simple: find a rock bigger than the one rolled by the last contestant and push it down the glacier. The rock that rolled the farthest won the game.

In 1963, BFH, Frank Maranville, and the usual Shelton climbing contingent, including Tom Needham, Dick Morton, my oldest sister, Mary, and several others, climbed the north ridge of Mount Adams in south-central Washington State. The trailhead at Killen Creek took the party up the pleasant few miles of alpine heather and firs to a large high bench of land at the base of the north ridge. BFH called this "Fly Camp," because sheep herds grazed the area and brought flies in profusion with them. The camp was otherwise comfortable and spectacular. From Fly Camp one could see the Pacific Ocean and all major peaks in the area. It also sat below the precipitous Adams Glacier, which bordered the west side of the north ridge. On the other side of the ridge was the equally impressive Lava Glacier.

We had a strong party, knew the keys to the north ridge route, and summited Adams by it at noon. The exit off the north ridge and slog across the broad crater of Mount Adams to the summit was a long one, about a mile and a half. BFH thus dubbed Adams "Old Misery" because of that seemingly endless walk to the top.

Figure 18 Near the top of Mount Adams North Ridge, 1960, with rime ice on the rocks.

The party made excellent time descending the ridge and took a long break in a flat rock notch about halfway down. Out of boredom, Needham casually kicked a grapefruit-sized rock off the ridge and watched it bounce for hundreds of feet, splashing the snow on the Lava Glacier. The Lava, a hanging glacier, was devoid of climbers below, so there was no risk to fauna.

## AVOIDING THE SUDDEN STOP

"Wow, look at that rock go!" Tom said. With that, Mount Adams shuffleboard was born. Morton, Mary, Tom, and I began a competition to see who could roll one the farthest. Of course no one took turns. We all grabbed the biggest rocks we could find and lobbed them off the ridge. In no time showers of rock were bouncing crazily, splashing onto the glacier and kicking up sprays of snow. Some of the rocks tumbled for a mile or more, even skipping over crevasses.

I found that if I threw a big flat rock and it gained enough momentum, it would "gyro," flip up on its edge and spin like a wheel. As such games tend to do, Mount Adams shuffleboard escalated.

"Here, George, help me lift this over to the edge," Needham said, putting his shoulder to a table-sized rock. *Wham, boom, crash, rattle,* followed by "Look at that baby go! Gawd, did you see that?"

"Needham, George, the rest of you, that's enough," BFH interjected. "We've had our fun here. Let's saddle up and get rolling."

From then on, no matter the climb, if it was safe to play Mount Adams shuffleboard, Needham made sure that we did. It was a kick—literally.

When the party arrived back at the Killen Creek trailhead, we found BFH's Plymouth station wagon blocked in by a Volkswagen Bug. BFH mustered the group. "We need to move this idiot's car."

The game must have gotten our mojo up, because a dozen of us found that the Bug moved quite easily. We dragged it out of the way.

"Hey, I've got an idea," Dick Morton said. "See that stump over there?" He pointed to a large flat-topped fir stump six feet away. "Why don't we put this thing up there? That will pay this clown the courtesy he paid us."

With newfound strength and enthusiasm, our party dragged the VW to the stump. "One, two, three, lift!" We placed the little car neatly on top. Its wheels hung two feet off the ground.

"Good trail art," Maranville remarked. We threw our gear into BFH's freed Plymouth station wagon, piled into our respective cars, and headed for home.

Moral: Don't block a car belonging to the Mount Adams shuffleboard team.

# 16 THE UNICORN

*"It's only sheet lightning."–BFH*

Unicorn Peak is the tallest of the Tatoosh Range. The Tatoosh consist of the "Alps" a viewer sees when looking south from the Paradise Inn The standard approach was via the Bench Lake, Snow Lake trailhead off the Stevens Canyon Road. Often, however, dad would make a longer day of it by climbing Plummer, Pinnacle, Castle, Unicorn Sister, and Unicorn peaks in a single easterly traverse, starting at the Pinnacle Peak trailhead near Reflection Lake. Unicorn Peak was one of BFH's favorite climbs. On my first trip to it in 1961, Maranville and Jerry Shimek accompanied BFH and me. On the trail near Snow Lake, Jerry looked up at the spectacular summit spire which gave the mountain its name.

Figure 19 Unicorn and Unicorn Sister.

"Wow, Frank, look at the summit of that thing," Jerry said to Maranville. "Can we all sit up there at once?"

"Probably not," Maranville opined. "I've heard tell that the summit up there is so small that when a climber sits down he can get only one cheek on it."

BFH, who had been listening in silence to the dialogue interjected: "So, are you trying to tell us that it's a half-assed mountain?"

One late summer's day when I was fourteen, the weather report forecasted rain, wind, and thunderstorms, so BFH chose to do the standard climb of Unicorn. The party that day was only a single rope of three: BFH, Catherine, and me. Hiking into Snow Lake, heavy rain showers developed. We stopped to eat at Snow Lake then began the hop up the boulder field forming the alluvial fan around the lake. At the notch above the lake we hit snowfields and roped up. BFH led, followed by Catherine and me. The temperature dropped dramatically as we climbed up toward the saddle between Unicorn Peak and Unicorn Sister. Wind rose to gusts and sleet and snow began to fall.

"You tell him," I said. Catherine, her blue nylon shell parka hood cinched snugly around her face, was conferring with me about continuing the climb. Knowing dad, I was more than skeptical of a yielding response.

"We are climbing into a nasty storm. I don't think we should go on." Catherine turned from me to BFH. "Dad, this is getting bad. I'm cold. Maybe we should go back."

"We're fine," BFH responded, continuing his upward plod. We reached the saddle and began the climbing traverse along the southeastern side of the ridgeline, which ended at Unicorn's vertical summit plug. *Boom!* Thunder shattered the air, followed closely by a flash. *Boom!*

"Hey, Dad," I said. "Catherine's hands are really cold, and this lightning looks dangerous. We should turn around."

BFH stopped, took off his pack, and fished out a pair of leather outer shell mittens. "Here, Catherine, put these on." As she did I could hear her teeth chattering.

"Dad, this is not good. Catherine's freezing, and I'm afraid to get on the top of Unicorn. It's a lightning rod in this storm."

"That's only sheet lightning," he said. "It doesn't strike the ground, only cloud to cloud."

"But, Dad," I protested, "the summit of this thing sticks up right in between the clouds."

"It'll go. We're almost there." He tossed his head toward the summit. "Just another rope length."

That last rope length on Unicorn Peak is the crux of the climb. The spine of the ridge approaching the summit peters out into a thin rock notch. Thus the "unicorn" part of Unicorn Peak stands by itself, with hundreds of feet of vertical exposure on all sides. Today, despite the conditions, BFH was pressing on. He waved me over. "George, belay me. There's one move up there that is dicey." It was also icy. Ice was building up on the rock. Snow flurries drove past us in gusts. BFH methodically edged into the last rock pitch. I had set up a sitting belay, but I knew that the farther BFH moved away, the less effective the belay would be. Slowly, BFH climbed up into the fog. About forty feet of rope had paid out. He was nearing the end of the slack in the gold line to Catherine, who was in the middle. I turned to Catherine.

"Your rope to Dad is almost used up." I grabbed her web sling waistband. "If Dad falls, he'll go off there." I pointed down the cliff under BFH's feet. "If he does, there's no way I can hold him with this." Catherine looked at my belay and nodded. "The only thing we can do if he falls is to jump down the left side of this ridge."

## AVOIDING THE SUDDEN STOP

I pointed down Unicorn's northwest cliff. Catherine knew. She nodded again, teeth chattering. *Boom!* A lightning flash lit up the cloud around BFH's murky form, inching its way to the top. He looked eerily biblical.

A couple of minutes later, he was out of sight. There came two quick tugs on the rope. BFH was on top and ready to belay us up. Up Catherine and I went, in turn slipping on the water-ice building up on the rock, but being held securely by BFH. *Crack! Wham! Boom!* We were on the top. I'd never felt more like a lightning rod. Panic was beginning to well up. "Dad, let's get out of here!" Catherine, her hands beginning to thaw, was moaning in pain. BFH agreed.

"Let's blow this cave," he said. "I don't want to take the time to set up a rappel. So I'll belay you and Catherine down the way we just came up, and you belay me down."

"OK," I said. "You ready?"

"Yes, go!" BFH was sitting in his belay position. I noticed that he was wearing only a woolen ear band. His head was completely iced up. I eased my feet over the edge.

My boots slipped off of most of the rock holds, so BFH essentially just lowered me. There was one consolation. The thunder and lightning was abating. I scrambled and yo-yoed down to the notch. Catherine soon followed, still moaning with the pain in her hands. This time I slid myself about twenty feet down the western cliff, found a couple of toeholds, and belayed BFH. It was more of a squatting belay, but at least I put the ridgeline between BFH and me. "Tell Dad he's on belay and can go," I yelled up to Catherine. She relayed the message, and slowly slack could be taken in on the gold line, indicating that BFH was down-climbing. At any instant I expected a shout of "Falling!" and the slam of rope coming taut. Could I hold him? Probably not, I thought. I concentrated on maintaining some semblance of a belay. What if dad fell, and the rope, now straining over the rocks, was cut? Dad would plunge down the east face, and I down the west. Catherine, now tied only to me, would be pulled off my side. I pushed back the welling fear, locked it up in a corner of my mind, and looked down, concentrating on my hands belaying the rope around my body. More slack was taken up. The thunder and lightning had moved on to the east toward Little Tahoma. The gray skies were getting lighter. It had stopped snowing.

Catherine waved. "Dad's here."

To this day I don't know how BFH made that climb down off the summit plug of Unicorn Peak without peeling off. But he did. I am sure my shoulder angel loomed large in the outcome.

"Catherine, take your gloves off and put your bare hands on your stomach under your clothes. You'll warm up your hands better that way."

"Ow," she choked. Tears streamed down her face.

We quickly got moving, dropping back to the saddle

bordering Unicorn Sister. Gradually the pain in Catherine's hands subsided, the clouds broke, and the sun came out. We glissaded the half mile down from the saddle to the notch above Snow Lake on four inches of new snow. By the time we boulder-jumped back to Snow Lake, Catherine's fingers had thawed and her pain dulled. The sun streamed out on the steaming lake.

"That was a good drill," BFH said. He then added, "I'm proud of you both. It was a tough go there for a while."

Indeed it was. BFH drove himself and us hard in the mountains in my early climbing days. I suppose it was a way to cull out the stress of his job and home. By this age I was seasoned and confident of my skills, even though at fourteen, I was still a very young mountaineer by the measure of that era. Mine were skills that had been tested, honed in the sharp unforgiving lessons of the sport, and in the adversity my father craved in it. I had earned them. Dropping back to walk alone, I pondered this on the trail out to the car from Snow Lake. Why did dad push this climb so far today? Did he have a death wish? If he did, he didn't care about the consequences to Catherine and me. I couldn't believe this was so.

I stopped to watch a ptarmigan hen and her chicks scurry across the trail. She squatted down a few feet away and her chicks ran under her. Animals protect their young.

Walking on, I could see across a long meadow. Dad

and Catherine were just moving around a corner as the trail angled down to the trailhead and the car. No, dad didn't really have a death wish. Maybe it was a don't-give-a-damn wish. That was more like it. Push things as far as you can up here and see what happens. And if you walk away at the end of the day you're just the better for it. That was more in line with dad's character. Plus, he was where he wanted to be—up here. He and mom were extremely unhappy in their marriage. He wanted to get a divorce, but was staying until I, the last of the kids, left for college. Dad had met mom up at Paradise in 1939. She had regularly taken the train or bus up there from Seattle, and he worked at the Inn and cabins. Strange. They were too much the same to get along. Both were talented. Both were self-centered. Both had college degrees, and BFH had gone on to law school at the University of Washington and a successful law career. Mom graduated from the U.W. as a dietician, but she never used her training. She wanted to teach in the Shelton schools but dad wouldn't let her. Any thought of a wife going to work was an assault on his pride. He was the breadwinner and in his household there would be only one. Maybe that was it. Maybe that's why they fought. I walked out of the trees into the parking lot. All the doors were open on our Plymouth station wagon, and the tailgate was down. BFH and Catherine were stowing their wet gear. It was my turn.

# 17 THE KNOT

*There's nothing quite as grand as a frozen double-overhand.*

My father, BFH, favored tying in to our climbing ropes with a loop hooked to a waistband carabiner. The waistband was a length of one-inch flat nylon tie-in ribbon wrapped three times around the waist, tied with a square knot on the third wrap, with loose ends tied off through the whole waistband with half-hitches. This configuration enhanced mobility, making it easy to get on and off the climbing rope by merely unclipping the waistband carabiner from the loop in the climbing rope. The knot we utilized for this loop was a double overhand. It was bulky, could be unwieldy at times, and was prone to freeze up in the cold and ice. This made it difficult to untie. Thus many climbers favored the figure-eight knot for main tie-in loops because it lay flatter and skinnier.

In early July of 1964, BFH and his climbing coleader, Frank Maranville, took a party of twelve on a climb of Little Tahoma on the eastern flank of Mount Rainier. This trip included my sister Catherine, and others from our hometown of Shelton, Washington. At fifteen, I was by now "seasoned," having climbed the major peaks of the Cascades, including Mount Rainier two years before, and many in the Olympics. This was also my third climb of Little Tahoma, which I had first summited in 1961 at age twelve, when I was issued my first pair of crampons.

The party camped at Summerland and departed for the summit in darkness with the use of headlamps. We climbed up to Meany Crest next to the Frying Pan Glacier, where we roped up. Bob Jeffery and Catherine were on a two-man team. I was leading another, and BFH and Frank Maranville were directing the party from the middle and rear ropes.

True to its name, the Frying Pan is a wide, flat glacier approaching Little Tahoma's precipitous east flank. However, it is slightly convex at its middle. This convexity can be vexing for route-finding, since crevasses, which normally run perpendicular to the fall line, can radiate in all directions, like cracks on an eggshell. The way was heavily crevassed. Several times, in order to find a route through them, BFH had our two two-man rope teams act as pathfinders. Bob and Catherine would explore one direction, and Tom Needham and I would probe another. Whichever team found the viable route would remain in the lead, and the other two-man team would fall in behind, along with the rest of the party. As we neared the middle of the Frying Pan, crevasses began to splay out at all angles. Route-finding became difficult even though the dawning day was clear and sunny, and we could see the access notch onto the Whitman Glacier to the west. This was the major waypoint where the route swung north and steepened toward the summit of Little Tahoma. But now we were being bottled up in a heavily crevassed area. I climbed off to the left with Needham. Bob and Catherine explored to the right.

Bob's voice came back, "I've found a snow bridge over here that will take us through."

"OK, Bob." I closed back within a few feet of Catherine. Neither of us could see Bob, but his rope was moving normally along the crusted snow up beyond a slight rise.

Catherine and I were chatting and walking along. All seemed normal, and Jeffery had not called back with an update on what he was doing. Behind me was Needham, behind him was BFH with his three-man team, with Maranville and the rest of our party following.

Suddenly Catherine exclaimed, "Oh!" and was yanked violently off her feet and pulled uphill by her rope. She was flailing and trying to self-arrest with her ice axe, but it wasn't working. In a blink she disappeared over the rise in the glacier and was gone. One second I was chatting with my sister; the next she had vanished. There was no sound. It was totally still.

For another instant I stood rooted in disbelief. Then it dawned on me what had occurred. I turned back toward BFH and choked out, "Bob has fallen into a crevasse, and I'm afraid that Catherine went in with him. She was just pulled up out of sight and I don't see how she could have stopped herself." My voice quavered.

"Can you see her?"

"No, Dad, I can't."

"Well, get on up there where you can." His voice was forceful, clinical.

It was the longest rope length of my life. I climbed quickly, but with each step I could see nothing but a trail of scrape marks in the snow. I was afraid to follow it. I kept walking. I began to top the rise and still there was no sign of my sister. I was being forced to be the first to observe a terrible tragedy and I fought against witnessing it.

"Dad, I still can't see Catherine. I think she's gone."

Again BFH called back a gruff command: "Keep going."

I did. Finally cresting the rise, I could now see a crevasse. It was fifteen-feet-wide. I traced Bob Jeffery's tracks meandering off to the left. They terminated on a broken snow bridge. I scanned to the right, along the white streaks of disturbed snow that marked my sister's slide and her frantic fight to stop it. There, stuck headfirst at the very edge of the crevasse, was Catherine. She was on her stomach, feet splayed behind her with the cramponed toes of her boots dug in.

I yelled back to BFH, "Dad, she's stuck right on the edge. She's alive!"

BFH, Maranville, and the rest of the party huffed up toward me. While I waited, I talked to my sister.

"Catherine, thank God you're here!"

"Thank God you're here," she said, looking back.

"Can you see Jeffery?"

"Yes." Her voice was remarkably composed. "He's hanging in midair at least a hundred feet below me."

"How do you know he's in midair and not at the bottom?"

"Because I'm looking straight down at him and he's spinning."

BFH, Maranville, and the rest of the party were now congregated near the crevasse.

BFH turned to Maranville. "Frank, move around and get a look at the sides of this thing. Catherine may be on an overhang."

A couple of minutes later Maranville called back forty feet from the left, "You're right, there's a big lip on this side and Catherine's on it." Catherine started to kick her feet into the snow.

"Dad, get me out!"

"OK, here's the deal, Catherine," BFH said, now in more soothing tones. "You are on a cornice. Don't kick. We have to get you secured somehow. I'm afraid to walk up to you because we could break the cornice." He paused, thinking. BFH was always thinking. Catherine stopped kicking.

"Can you breathe?"

"Yes, but I'm stuck, the rope is pulling on my waistband, and it hurts." BFH turned to my teammate Tom Needham.

"Tom, get a boot-axe belay on George and take in the slack." Needham rammed the shaft down into the hard snow and set a belay on me.

"George, you're as light as anyone here." BFH took off his pack, unclipped from his rope, unhooked a second carabiner from his waist sling, and snapped it into the loop. He looked at me over his sunglasses. His eyes were intense, serious.

"Take this loop, lay down as flat as you can, and when I tell you, belly crawl out to Catherine. You have to snap this carabiner here on the end of my rope into your sister's waistband. That's the only way we can take the weight off of her and get her stabilized."

I got down on my knees with the rope, took a deep breath, and prepared to crawl.

"Give me your ice axe," BFH said. "Crawling out there you won't need it. You're already on belay." I handed him my axe. BFH's reasoning was impeccable, but now I felt even more exposed. Ice axes on ice are comfort blankets.

BFH turned around to Maranville, who was now back among us.

"Frank, take your team and find a way around this

thing. We're going to need you and some horsepower on the other side. Since the lip of the crevasse is corniced over here, you will have to get another rope down to Bob for him to step into. We'll set up a bulgari rescue. When Bob is brought up near this lip, you will pull him toward you so we can work him up and over this thing."

Maranville was already on his way. He and BFH had climbed together for many years. They read each other's minds.

"How are you doing, Catherine?" I asked.

"I want out of this."

"I'm way back here and I want out of this too. I can't imagine what it's like for you. But you're doing great. We'll get you out. Hang in there, sister." She was—literally.

"What's Bob doing?"

"He's been spinning around upside down, but he's just pulled himself upright and he's standing in his prusik sling," she reported, adding, "he's really far down there." The prusik sling is a chest-length rope with loops at both ends. One loop serves as a stirrup for a boot, and the other is tied onto the climbing rope in a prusik hitch. When the prusik hitch is slid up the rope as the foot in the stirrup loop is raised, the knot binds, allowing a climber to step up and relieve pressure off the rope around his waist.

"OK, George, the rope in your hand is now on belay." BFH had set up party members behind me to anchor it. "Go."

I got down on my belly and slowly, methodically, belly-crawled. It was cold. The morning sun had not yet heated the air on the Frying Pan, but I was sweating profusely. Fifteen feet. Ten feet.

"I can feel myself moving!" Catherine yelled, her voice raised in fear for the first time. I froze and waited. I couldn't feel movement, so slowly I again inched forward, fighting off panic and the cascading, numbing mental projections: of the cornice breaking off, of my sister falling into the crevasse, of chunks of snow following her into the void, of Bob Jeffery spinning helplessly in the cold, dark hole more than one hundred feet below. Would she scream? If she did would I hear her?

"Get moving, George." BFH's voice snapped me back. I took a deep breath and inched forward. Five feet. Four.

"Stop!" Catherine shouted. "I'm moving!" BFH heard her.

"George, if you reach out you can grab her boots. Slip the loop around them and snap the carabiner back on the rope."

"But, Dad, if I do that and the lip breaks off Catherine will be pulled apart."

"Do it," came the flat reply.

Catherine understood. She slid her boots together, I cinched the rope around them, and the belay team brought the rope tight. That was the best we could do at the moment.

"Frank," BFH yelled across the crevasse, "flip the

end of a rope down to Bob with a loop in it. Tell him to thread it through his waistband like he's done with his prusik sling and step into it. You set up a belay station there and we'll bulgari him up." The bulgari rescue encompasses setting up a rope with a stirrup end for both of the victim's feet, and separate belayers for both feet up on top. At the command "Raise the right foot," slack developed by raising it is retrieved and held by the "right foot" belayer. The victim can then step up and be held on that rope. "Raise the left foot," is followed in similar fashion by the belayer for the left foot. This is repeated, gradually lifting the victim safely out of the crevasse.

Maranville nodded, tossed a looped end of gold line into the hole, and placed an ice axe shaft at right angles to the rope at the top of the crevasse on his side to keep friction from sawing it too far into the snow as it was pulled up. Maranville had a better look at Bob on his side and could yell down to him.

Bob Jeffery, spinning in the dark, felt as though he was a continent away. The remnants of the snow bridge that had broken out from under him had silently disappeared somewhere below. He switched on his headlamp and looked down between his feet. The light did not reach the bottom. Bob knew that he was dangling at 120 feet, because this was the length of the braided gold line that ran between Catherine and him. Since he could look straight up and see Catherine's head, now made small by the distance, he knew that the rope that finally jerked him to a stop had used up the last inches of its full length. How in the world had Catherine stopped? He wondered, especially since she was headfirst up there looking down at him. The way the fall had occurred, had she executed a self-arrest he would be looking at her feet instead of her head. Bob may have been baffled at being alive, but it didn't keep him from being glad of it. He took a deep breath and waited.

Maranville's muffled voice drifted down, breaking the silence. Another rope snaked down next to him. It had a big loop tied in its end. Minutes earlier, Bob had been hanging upside down. He had managed to right himself and pull the free end of his manila prusik sling out of his pants pocket. The prusik was a body length of half-inch Manila line with stirrups braided into each end. One of the loop-stirrups tied into the climbing rope with a prusik knot. The other end had been passed through the waistband, and the other stirrup stashed in his pocket. This setup was precisely the remedy for Bob's current predicament. It was now time to use it. Bob put his boot into the free stirrup, bent his right leg, slid the prusik knot up the climbing rope, and stepped up. The cutting weight on his waistband was now relieved and transferred to his foot. Step one, he thought.

"Bob, grab this rope, run the loop through your waistband, and put your left boot in it. OK, good. Now lift your left leg. We've got you on belay up here, so all you have to do is raise your leg. We'll take in the slack, and you can step up on it."

## AVOIDING THE SUDDEN STOP

Bob understood. He had practiced the bulgari crevasse rescue technique on glacier training days with Maranville and BFH. He was surprised how easily the procedure came back to him. He lifted up a long athletic leg and stepped up. In that first step, Bob made it possible to save Catherine. Maranville nodded over to BFH on our side of the crevasse.

"Bob has his weight now fully transferred to our rope. Go ahead and pull Catherine back from the edge." BFH told our belay team to pull. The gold line around Catherine's feet cinched tighter. She was jerked a couple of inches back. "Good!" BFH said. "Catherine, use your ice axe and carefully push back as we pull." This time she came back another six inches. Then another foot. Then two feet.

"George, she's back far enough from the cornice now. You crawl out there with this." BFH tossed me another length of gold line with a loop and carabiner on it. This time, with the enthusiasm born of hope's glimmer, I crawled quickly, reached out, and heard the reassuring click of the carabiner snapping the rescue rope into the taut nylon ribbon on Catherine's waistband. I gave it a tug to make sure. Catherine pushed her way back toward us as the party on her side of the crevasse pulled her and took in the slack. A few more feet and she could unclip from Bob's rope and stand up for the first time in over an hour.

"Good job, daughter. Move back and take a break." BFH patted her on the back.

Bob Jeffery wasn't saved yet, but he was getting closer. Up he slowly went, one or two feet with each raise of a leg. Raise the right leg. Feel the slack taken in. Step up. Raise the left leg. Feel the slack taken up. Ninety feet—sixty—forty.

Maranville, now coordinating the rescue, called to BFH, "Bob's coming nicely right up the middle of the crevasse." Twenty feet. Fifteen.

Bob Jeffery's head appeared over the cornice.

"Take it easy now." Maranville held up a hand to stop the belay teams from pulling. "I'll pay out a little slack from my side. Bob, use your axe to chop a bigger hole there in the cornice so you can get through. Be careful not to chop your rope." Jeffery hacked away for a few minutes, opening a hole in the crevasse lip wide enough for his shoulders to pass. Maranville gave a thumbs-up. We gave a shout and a yank, and Jeffery popped over the edge next to us.

Figure 20 Practicing the bulgari rescue technique on the Nisqually Glacier, Mount Rainier. Frank Maranville is the "Victim" being pulled from the crevasse.

BFH and Maranville conferred, looking over Catherine's double-overhand tie-in knot.

"It was the bulk of this knot that jammed into the

lip and stopped her."

"I agree," Maranville said. "No doubt about it. If she hadn't tied in with a double overhand today there's a strong chance that neither Catherine nor Bob would be standing here with us now. When Bob broke through the snow bridge and dragged Catherine uphill, friction caused the rope to burn its way several feet into the cornice before the knot came to it and stuck."

We rested. Bob and Catherine both looked beat. BFH and Maranville conferred again, glancing at their watches.

"It's only eight thirty," BFH said. "It took us an hour and forty-five minutes to do this rescue. We were an hour ahead of schedule before Bob fell in. Everything was going well."

"So, we only really lost forty-five minutes," Maranville replied, completing BFH's thought.

"We have plenty of time; the weather is good. We are past the worst part of this route, and I can see a good path all the way to notch on the Whitman Glacier." BFH pointed for emphasis. "We can be there in an hour and go on to complete this climb."

"Bob and I don't want to go on. We want to go back," Catherine said.

"I understand how you feel," Maranville replied quietly. "Both of you have had a close call. But neither of you are hurt and both of you are strong. Grab a bite to eat, a salt pill, and some water, and you'll feel better when you start again."

"The two of you are going to have to walk this off in some direction, no matter what. It might as well be up," added BFH.

Catherine, Bob, and the rest of our party did walk it off. Mostly. We summited and completed the climb of Little Tahoma. Catherine and Bob Jeffery never climbed again. That is understandable. At least with the help of a big bulky double overhand knot tied with seven-sixteenth inch gold line nylon rope, they were able to walk away from a big crevasse fall on the Frying Pan Glacier. They avoided the sudden stop. For that I am forever grateful. And so is Tom Needham. He later married Catherine.

# 18 Welcome to Sumner, Washington

*"Now for the most dangerous part of the climb, the drive home."* –BFH

The Shelton climbing group led by BFH and Frank Maranville mustered at the White River Campground for a trip up the Emmons Glacier. A significant participant on this climb was Louis Stur, western editor for Summit magazine and manager of the Challenger Inn at Sun Valley, Idaho. Louis and his mother and sister had fled the Soviet invasion of Hungary in 1956 and emigrated to the United States and Idaho. There Louis quickly built a climbing reputation with Jerry Fuller and Fred Beckey, putting in several technical first ascents in the Sawtooth Range. Stur was also an acclaimed glider pilot and soaring instructor, notable for being the only instructor in the United States who did not hold a license for powered flight. He once strapped me in for a spectacular glider ride out of the Hailey Airport one sparkling summer's day in 1964.

On this trip, I was tapped to be on a two-man rope with Louis. Our first night on the Emmons route was spent in the meadows of Glacier Basin. The next day we proceeded up the Inter Glacier to Camp Schurman, at the top of Steamboat Prow, circa 9,500 feet. In the mid-1960s the Schurman Hut, which had been privately built by the Mountaineers, was open for private parties on a first-come basis. It had not yet been commandeered by the Park Service. There were fifteen in our party, but by leaving most of our gear outside, we all squeezed into the hut to sleep.

BFH began the summit climb at precisely one o'clock in the morning. The Emmons Glacier route is akin in exposure to the old Mount Saint Helens. The angle is generally consistent at thirty-five degrees. The problem, as with Mount Saint Helens, is that the fall line extends for miles, "to the oyster beds," as BFH would say. This makes for significant exposure. Many climbers have died on the Emmons as a result. The route demands respect like any other on a big mountain, but the manageable incline of the Emmons Glacier can dull perceptions of the hazards.

Louis Stur led the party. Louis was a climber in the

grand European tradition. Reserved and elegant in demeanor, Louis moved with easy grace. He was also a grand mentor.

"George, see how the snow color changes over there? That is a hidden crevasse. Be sure to probe with your axe before crossing, or better yet, go around on the ice over there." Louis had a perennial smile. He talked amiably as we climbed, interspersing instructive comments with stories of his past climbs.

"George, one day in the late 1950s, Fred Beckey drove over to visit me at Sun Valley. He wanted to do only first ascents, and I knew the peaks that hadn't yet been climbed. One day, on a beautiful vertical spire above Red Fish Lake in the Stanley Basin, Fred climbed within twenty feet of the summit. I was belaying him from a rock piton below. Suddenly I hear this terrible swearing. A few minutes later, Fred rappelled down to me. He was very angry. 'Louis, I thought you said this was unclimbed.' 'Yes, I believe so, Fred,' I said. 'Well, that's bullshit. I just ran into a piton on the last pitch!' Beckey insisted on going down immediately. I said, 'Fred, it is a beautiful day on a beautiful rock. Why don't we complete the last few feet of this climb?' Well, George, Beckey never answered. He just rappelled off the peak and walked away. Summits didn't interest Fred on that day. Only first summits," Louis reflected with a wry smile and a wink.

We were up at the bergschrund at 13,200 feet by nine that morning. I looked back down the long strands of gold line and plodding figures of BFH, Maranville, Rich Brewer, and others in our party. Dick Vanderflute, a good friend of BFH and the manager of the Paradise Ski School, was fiddling with his Mamiya RB67 large-format camera. It came with several interchangeable backs, or cassettes, like a Hasselblad, which held different types of film. Dick would take some fine photos on this day.

Figure 21 Brian O'neil, Louis Stur, and the author at Camp Schurman, 1965.

"George," Louis interrupted my observations. "Come up here." He coiled in the one hundred twenty feet of rope between us and I cramponed up beside him. We were standing on the flat bottom lip of the bergschrund. Louis handed me back his coils.

"Now, George, see that nice blue snow bridge here in front of us? I want you to go off to the right, look at it from the side, and tell me if you think it is stable." I walked to the side and glanced under the bridge. There was white crusted snow on its top, but starting a foot down, and extending fifteen feet into the big crevasse, was a span of solid blue ice. Icicles hung off its edges.

"It looks good for crossing," I said.

"I agree. George, come on back to me. I am going to carefully cross it. You give me protection." I started to set a boot-axe belay. "George, for this, all you need is a shoulder belay. Stand right up here." Louis took me to the edge of the crevasse. "Now do a shoulder belay. Just put one strong leg a little forward. Good!"

"But, Louis, this feels precarious," I said worriedly.

"No, it is very strong, George. It is how we do it in the Alps. Just pay the rope out as I cross, and give me just a little slack. If you see me fall, stand straight, and let your back and legs take the force." With that, and a reassuring nod, Stur gingerly probed his way across the snow bridge. He never looked back. He trusted me completely. Our route then angled north toward the top of the Winthrop Glacier and entered the saddle between Liberty Cap, the north peak Mount Rainier.

BFH's party summited at eleven o'clock, climbing directly to Columbia Crest, past the remnants of the old crater. Louis Stur bowed and shook hands all around, in old-world style. The descent of the Emmons went well, but it was a long way back to the parking lot at the White River Campground. When we finally dragged in there at six, BFH was happy. We had a good climb with great company. "Now for the most dangerous part of the trip—the drive back to Shelton," BFH quipped.

Frank Maranville was a bad driver. No one wanted to ride with him, so we often used his 1962 Rambler station wagon as "the equipment vehicle." Gear was stuffed in everywhere, thus precluding occupants. Somehow, however, Maranville had rearranged things. "I have room for two here in the backseat," he said as he opened the door. Rich Brewer and I were unfortunate enough to be the closest. "Hop in!"

I don't know whether the steering was loose on the Rambler or whether it was Maranville. Yes, I do know. It was Maranville. He never actually steered his car around a corner. Negotiating a curve was always a series of hard jerks on the wheel. Since he was a scientist, we thought, maybe cornering was an experiment in the least movement of the steering wheel until the last possible moment. What resulted was not a cornering of the Rambler, but a maniacal swerving. Maranville and his Rambler created more terror for his riders than they'd experienced on the climbs. Hence, Rich and I felt the hairs rise on the backs of our necks as we drove the winding two-lane road out of the park. Having survived exiting the park, we decided to get some sleep. The flatlands would be straighter.

"Look out!" Brewer's scream rang out a pubescent double octave. I sprang up, and there directly in front of the Rambler's windshield stood a huge brown wooden sign with bright white letters: "Welcome to Sumner,

Washington, A Happy Town." Now I did a double octave. Maranville cranked the steering wheel violently to the right. The Rambler skidded sideways. We were doing sixty miles per hour on the grassy shoulder of the road. In the side-view mirror I could see huge chunks of turf being gouged out of the shoulder from the sliding wheels. Just as I braced for impact with the sign, the Rambler fishtailed around it with inches to spare. We were back on the freeway now, and Maranville was motoring merrily along in the fast lane. The bouncing, the shifting of climbing gear in the back, and our terror, subsided. Maranville's tired face, with remnants of clown-white sunscreen still streaked on it, smiled back into the rearview mirror. "I think I fell asleep for a second there," he said with an embarrassed shrug.

Brewer and I tag-teamed the rest of the way home, keeping Maranville awake with commentary-inducing questions. Brewer asked the best one, which spawned an hour's good response: "Dr. Maranville, why is the sky blue?" We arrived in Shelton. The most dangerous part of the climb—driving home with Maranville—ended.

When we returned to Mount Rainier for a hike some weeks later, the gouge marks and long strips of broken turf still reposed there by the sign, brown and dried out. Welcome to Sumner.

# 19  The Hidden Crevasse

*"I thought he was dead."* –BFH

"It's a clear day." Tim Pinkney sat up from his sleeping bag in the back of my mustard-colored 1968 GMC van. "What do you think, George, should I wear my long john bottoms?"

I looked out the window. We were parked at the trailhead above Spirit Lake. The sun was just touching the top of the Forsythe Glacier. It looked to be a hot day, maybe a cooker, if there was no breeze. "Yes, Tim, put them on. It will be warm, but you can tolerate the heat better from the waist down. And if you end up in a crevasse, it will be cold regardless." Pinkney nodded and put them on. I always wore mine.

BFH and the rest of the Shelton climbing party arrived at the trailhead at seven that morning. BFH was in his sixties then and had sworn off camping. "I'd rather sleep in my own bed, get up earlier, and make the drive," he'd say.

We donned our gear, trudged up the pumice approaches, and roped up on the Forsythe. I was on a two-man rope with my old buddy Jerry Shimek. Pinkney, a newbie to climbing, was roped between BFH and Roger Lovett. The trip up Saint Helens was classic, straightforward. There was a small icefall to be negotiated next to the top of the Dog's Head, but it posed no problems. BFH and his party were in good shape and spirits. The false summit was reached by eleven thirty and the summit by noon. We had lunch sitting among the wreckage of the old abandoned fire lookout.

"We'll descend by the Dog's Head route," BFH declared.

By the time our party started down at one thirty in the afternoon, the snow was getting sloppy. Other parties were on the mountain, but they were well spread out. Shimek and I had just left the false summit at the north end of the Saint Helens crater when a jogger in shorts loped past us. Running merrily behind him was his pet Saint Bernard.

Strange, I thought to myself. Here we are all roped and geared up, and this fellow just moseys up and down the mountain with his dog, ignoring the crevasses and other hazards. God protects such people and their dogs.

## AVOIDING THE SUDDEN STOP

Figure 22 BFH looks toward the camera as a jogger and his Saint Bernard dog (below), ran by our rope teams.

Though the snow was soft, it plunged well. Looking down the long fall line toward the top of the Dog's Head, I viewed a widening trail of descending tracks. This is common, because the plunged steps of others are like post holes to those following, so people tend to walk just outside the previous climbers' tracks. This bodes risk. Anytime boots deviate from the established route on a glacier, they are essentially walking an untested route. Many climbers have been killed by falling through hidden crevasses in this manner.

Shimek and I had just reached the Dog's Head and were beginning to unrope. I looked up to see BFH pacing nervously back and forth next to a small dark hole about two hundred yards up the glacier. "Jerry, someone fell in. We've got to get up there."

By the time we raced to the spot, BFH had already lowered Lovett into the crevasse. "Pinkney's down there," BFH said.

I looked into the hole. Twenty feet down I saw a single hand sticking out of the snow. It had an ice axe in it. My heart sank. Pinkney had cut the corner of a hidden crevasse ever so slightly, but enough to step onto the thinnest crust. The crust broke off a coffin-sized slab of snow, Pinkney fell in, and the wet sun-softened slab fell on top of him.

"Tim, can you hear me?" I shouted, dubious. The hand with the axe waved. "Hey, Dad, Tim can breathe," I said. "He waved his axe. He must have trapped an air pocket down there."

BFH nodded.

"OK, Dad, get the rest of our party set up for a rescue. I need another rope down there. And let's move fast, because I don't know how much air Pinkney's got left trapped under that snow."

I looked back down into the hole. Roger Lovett was braced up against one side of the narrow crevasse. He was a novice climber too, and a look in his eyes told me he was out of his element. I could pull Roger out and go down there myself, but that would take time, and BFH hadn't set up belays yet. Looking at Tim's hand sticking out of the snow, axe in hand, posed a problem. How was he situated? I could see no other part of him. By his hand's orientation, palm up, I knew roughly where his head was. Was he supine or sitting? I looked back at his hand and over at his rope. The gold line disappeared into the white debris about six feet away.

## AVOIDING THE SUDDEN STOP

"Roger, here's the deal," I said. "You need to dig Pinkney out. And we need to do it quickly, but in the right way. Initially I don't want you to dig next to Tim's head. Doing that could hurt him or collapse his air pocket." Roger nodded tentatively. "Take the adz-end of your ice axe and start digging where Tim's rope goes into the snow. Follow the rope to him."

Roger started scraping out snow at the rope end. He was moving too slowly. "Roger, what's the matter?"

"I don't feel comfortable. I feel like I'm going to fall."

I glanced back at BFH. All ropes were belayed. "It's natural to feel that way, Roger. You're on belay and not going anywhere. You may feel awkward and off balance, but you need to dig—now."

Roger went at it with a will. The problem was that he was chipping out the sides of the crevasse and not following the rope. "Roger, stop. Dig up the rope, not on the side of the crevasse! Do it now!" He finally got the message. Slowly more of the rope appeared. Pinkney would periodically wave his axe to indicate that he was still breathing—always a good sign. Thirty minutes went by. Pinkney's waist appeared. He was trapped in a partial sitting position. "Put the ice axe down and use your hands to pull snow away from Tim's chest and face." Minutes seemed an eternity, but Tim Pinkney was finally freed, and the party horsed him out. Then we brought up Roger.

Taking stock at the edge of the small blue hole, I noticed Tim was shivering. I retrieved my big orange Thaw down parka out of my pack and put him in it.

"I was beginning to freeze down there," Tim said. "When I fell, the snow was all slush, but it soon began to freeze into ice." He cast a glance in the direction of the hidden crevasse. His face was ash-white.

Figure 23 Tim Pinkney's first look at daylight after falling into the crevasse. Roger Lovett and the author are looking down, as Pinckney is finally uncovered.

The party gathered up, walked to the Dog's Head, unroped, and glissaded down toward the parking lot. As we descended, I stayed next to Pinkney. He had warmed up and the color had returned to his face. "Tell me about it, Tim," I said.

"I was coming down with your dad behind me and Roger in front. I decided to move to the new snow just to the left of the footprints. Then I suddenly dropped through the snow to my waist. My feet were dangling in thin air. I leaned forward, trying to spread my weight out. When I did that it must have acted like a lever, because a whole slab broke with me in the middle of it.

I dropped in and got wedged into a sitting position between the sides of the crevasse. Then all the snow landed on top of me and I couldn't move. Luckily the crevasse continued on down and a lot of the snow followed it and left enough space for me to breathe." Tim took a deep breath as we stepped out on the asphalt of the parking lot next to my mustard-colored van. "I'm glad you had me put on the long johns. It got real cold there toward the last."

BFH walked up and slapped Tim on the back. "You walked away from it, Pinkney. Good job."

"Man, Mr. Heuston, that was a close one."

BFH put his head down then looked up. "It was a good drill," he said.

Decades later my father further reflected: "When I looked into that crevasse and saw that Tim was trapped and covered with snow, I thought he was gone. If I'd have lost him on that day I would have quit the sport." Dad would have—but shoulder angels and luck enabled Tim to walk away—and BFH to continue climbing.

# 20  The Movie

*"Let's impress the girls."* –T. Needham

My first ascent of Mount Baker was memorable for two reasons. The first was that I had never seen such huge crevasses as graced the Coleman Glacier. The second was that a couple of us in the party failed miserably at a filming debut.

BFH and Frank Maranville ran the climb and rope teams in usual fashion. It was primarily a Shelton-Olympia party. I recall my high school locker partner and climbing buddy Mike Banner was along, as were Tom Needham and my sister Catherine.

Good weather led to a wonderful climb up the Coleman. We threaded through huge crevasses, some big enough to easily house two- or three-story buildings. The summit was reached by the standard route by eleven o'clock, and we took in the sights. The deep steaming crater yawned several hundred feet below. Sulfur fumes wafted the nose. Ten miles to the north stood the beautiful Mount Shuksan, whose likeness was long used as the cover photo on calendars. To the south were Mount Rainier, Adams, and Saint Helens, dominating the blue hazy spine of the Cascades.

We returned down the Roman Wall and Coleman Glacier the same way we ascended. The loose afternoon snow balled up in crampons and had to be beaten free with the shafts of our ice axes. Snow bridges were gingerly crossed over crevasses hundreds of feet deep. In those moments I willed myself to be lighter. By 1965 mountaineering in the Northwest had exploded in popularity; no longer did we have mountains to ourselves. On this day, other parties were on Baker, numbering upwards of eighty climbers besides ours of fifteen.

Back at high camp, just beyond the tree line above Kulshan Cabin, we coiled up the gold line, strapped on our sleeping bags and ground pads, and set out for the trailhead. Back on the trail, our party broke up into meandering clusters. Tom and I remained together. As I took a long step down to a tuft of grass, I felt a rip travel up the backside of the old knickers I was wearing. "Tom, take a look," I said.

"Geez, George it's huge!" Tom laughed. "It's a tear in your butt seam a good six inches long. I can see your underwear!"

"Let's stop for a minute. I'll get the pin." I dropped

my pack and unhooked a long steel safety pin from my shoulder strap. BFH swore by these in cases of such malfunctions.

"OK, Tom, take this and close the break in the pants," I instructed.

"Stand still!"

"Tom, if you jab me with that I'm going to chase you to the car."

"I won't jab you, but you gotta stand still. Bend over a little more." Tom was trying to suppress a laugh.

He threaded the needle of the big pin vertically, catching both sides of the torn inseam. I felt the safety hook latch.

"OK, I think I mostly got it," Tom said. "But there's still some underwear showing, and you may feel a little wind up your ass."

A few hundred yards into the tree line we approached a clearing. There, camped with their tents neatly in a row, was a group of young ladies. Some were quite good-looking, at least on that day. They were in brown uniforms, and a flag draped over a tent said: "Girl Scout Troop 1775" in bright yellow letters. An older lady, obviously the leader, was filming the girls and campsite with her eight-millimeter movie camera.

"George, let's walk through their camp."

"No, Tom, that lady is filming."

"That's just it. We'll walk through and she'll notice we're climbers and film us."

"No way, Tom. I'm not walking through that group

of girls with a safety pin up my butt and my underwear hanging out."

"It depends on how long they've been camped there," Tom said, "They may find you attractive."

"Shut up Tom," I retorted.

"Heck, George, they won't even notice it. I'll go first." Tom was off, not waiting for an answer.

I could have circumvented the scene by walking through the brush. But the trail ran right through the middle of the meadow and camp, and I was too tired to detour. I caught up to Tom. He was right. When the troop leader saw us emerging from the trees in our climbing gear she swung the camera around. Tom pulled himself up to a swagger, and I hunched down behind him the best I could. Needham got to the camp, waved to the camera, and promptly pitched headlong into an old fire pit. I nearly tripped over him. He had caught his foot on a rock of the fire ring. I looked down to see him all blackened, writhing around and trying to get up. His frame pack had flipped up over his head and now had him entangled. I quickly reached down, baring my backside, and scooped Needham up. He had mildly sprained his ankle. I could hear the movie camera whirring.

"Run!" Needham yelled as I scooted off like a striped ape, with Tom limping and covered in ashes trying to keep up.

"Gawd!" Tom exploded in giggles. "She got that whole thing on film!"

"Yes, she did, Tom. All of it, with you falling, getting

up covered in ashes, and limping away."

"And of you, George, with a safety pin up your ass. Gawd!"

We broke up laughing all the way to the car as Needham endlessly retold the episode, each time adding, "I wonder what they thought? Gawd!"

Somewhere in the archives of Girl Scout Troop 1775, there resides a grainy eight-millimeter movie capturing two intrepid climbers descending from Mount Baker. They have it to this day. They must. It was a keeper.

## 21 BALL BEARINGS

*"I couldn't look anymore. I headed down with the Doc." –BFH*

Mount Borah is the highest peak in Idaho at 12,667 feet. It ascends over five thousand feet in three and a half miles. In 1967, BFH, my uncle, Dr. Paul Heuston, his colleagues, Dr. Jim Earle and Jim Ball, and I, climbed by way of the standard ridge route to a high notch.

Dr. Earle looked at the last few rock pitches and balked. Perhaps this was understandable that he did, because that last part of the climb is called "Chicken Out Ridge." Its skinny spine sports airy drop-offs on each side, and the rock is unstable in spots.

From the notch, BFH remained with Dr. Earle and watched the rest of us summit and start back down.

However, we took a "shortcut" down the west face.

"Uncle Paul, why don't we just climb back to the notch to Dad and Dr. Earle?" I asked.

"Because the rock pitch down to it is tough."

"But we climbed up it fine." Paul looked at me nonplussed.

"This will be a good shortcut. Follow me."

I glanced down to the notch and could make out BFH and Dr. Earle. They were watching us. I followed Ball and my uncle.

The west face of Mount Borah is not steep, per se. Apart from a few tricky moves on a couple of high-angle rock slabs, it plunged down at a constant thirty to thirty-five degrees. But it went on for fifteen hundred vertical feet. At first we climbed down roped together, but as we picked our way down the face it became evident that there was no place to arrest a fall.

"We might as well unrope," Uncle Paul said. "It's not going to do us any good here." I threw the coiled gold line over my shoulder and followed.

It was chilly in the high air, but I began to sweat profusely as we descended the down-angled granite slabs covered with pea gravel. This created a hairy situation where we had to avoid walking over ball bearings. My uncle Paul was not as experienced as BFH. He did not keep us together. I looked to see Jim Ball and my uncle a hundred feet below. They did not glance back at me—they watched only for themselves. A flash of anger welled up, mixing with my fear, and knotted like a hot

## AVOIDING THE SUDDEN STOP

ball in my chest. I thought about yelling down to the two men, but I didn't. I had to focus.

"OK, George, you're on your own here," I muttered to myself. "Take your time. Don't worry about anyone

Figure 24 The author on the desolate approach to Mount Borah, Idaho.

else, just yourself. Concentrate on each step. Kick the ball bearings out of the way, then place your boot. Good. Now the next one..."

I "cleaned" my way slowly, painfully, down the west face of Borah. To slip was to die. Time crept by. Shadows lengthened on the ridges. My boot caught on one piece of gravel and started to slip. "George, you're almost off this thing," I said aloud to myself. "Concentrate. You screwed up there and lost it. You allowed the ball bearings under your boot. Watch, scrape, place. Watch, scrape, place. Focus. You're almost there. Don't lose it now."

Finally I was off the last few feet of the face and joined Uncle Paul and Jim Ball on the boulder field at the bottom. My wool shirt was drenched in sweat.

"You were too slow," Uncle Paul said. "It's getting late, and we have to traverse under this big buttress on the left to get back to the ridge trail."

"Uncle Paul," I shot back, "you made the decision to take this shortcut. I made the decision to survive it. If I was too slow for you that's too bad." He scowled. I scowled back. With that we traversed into a fading light. I was the only one carrying a flashlight, and I gave it to my uncle to route-find around the buttresses adjoining the ridge, our objective. At least on this part of the descent we stayed together. The buttresses were much broader at the bottom than anticipated, and it lengthened our walk. Darkness closed in. Wind came up. It was now eight o'clock, and we still hadn't hit the ridge trail.

"Uncle Paul, I'm going to get my whistle out. Maybe we can reach Dad." I dug out my survival whistle and blew on it every few seconds as we walked. Nothing. I kept blowing. Finally, twenty minutes later, a faint two-finger whistle was heard in return. It was followed by BFH's voice hollering, "Yo! Over here!" We followed intermittent calls until finally we were reunited on the trail.

"Boy, Dad, it's good to see you!" I said.

"Likewise," he said.

"Paul, you took your time getting here," BFH said

to his brother.

"George was too slow," Paul said.

"I have a different view of it," BFH responded. "George made it down admirably *by himself* up there. And your 'shortcut' burned you." Dad was ready to light into his brother for his faulty judgment, and for turning his back on me; and his comment signaled disdain.

Paul wisely said nothing. He could well tell that his older brother was angry. Dad turned and led off down the trail. The party stuck tightly together so as to harvest light from BFH's flashlight to see where we could place our feet. In another half hour a beam from dad's light caught the reflection of a taillight on Paul's Jeep. I had avoided another sudden stop.

I collapsed in my uncle's 1960 Willys station wagon and slept the whole drive home. The jarring of the Jeep over ruts and rocks in the long dirt road went unnoticed in the sweet oblivion of an exhausted sleep.

Later, BFH told me that he'd understood the peril as he watched me pick my way down the face of Mount Borah.

"After a while I couldn't look anymore. I could see you peeling off at any time," he said. A fleeting concern etched his face. "So Doc Earle and I left the notch and headed down the ridge. I stopped about where I thought your traverse would intersect us. We waited several hours. I was just about to pull the plug and go get help when I heard your whistle. That was fortunate."

It *was* fortunate. I carried that little plastic emergency whistle in my first-aid pouch. I had never used it before, and I haven't used it since that long ball-bearing day on Borah. However, it remained always and faithfully in my gear ever after. It more than earned its place.

## 22  The Pack Board

*Put it on. It will stiffen both your resolve and your back.*

During one of his winters at the Paradise Inn in the 1930s, BFH built a pack board out of a pair of old hickory skis. It was uncomfortable and heavy.

"I once carried a hundred and twenty pounds of Baby Ruth candy bars on that old pack board from Longmire to Paradise," he said.

The pack board's shoulder straps were narrow, unpadded leather that bit into the shoulders. To help take weight off of them, BFH fashioned a tump line. This was a nylon cord with one end attached to the middle crosspiece of the pack board. The other end hooked into a broad headband loop. The tump line was placed on the victim's head after the pack board was shouldered, and adjusted so that the head could be used to bear part of the load. All this accomplished was to add a headache to sore shoulders.

BFH was proud of his creation. So proud that he had me carry it into base camps on climbs as I grew older and stronger. I was fourteen, had put on weight and muscle, and I sensed that dad had been "saving" the pack board for me as a rite of passage. It was my turn to carry the candy bars. I didn't like it, but there it was. My climbing companions, including BFH, carried new aluminum frame packs into base camps. They were supremely more comfortable by comparison, because they shifted the bulk of the carrying weight from the shoulders and back to a big padded cinch strap on the hips. To don one properly it was put on with the shoulder straps bearing the weight. Then the bearer shrugged his shoulders up while snuggly cinching the waist band. When he dropped his shoulders, the load was now primarily carried over the hips. This also lowered the load's center of gravity and provided better balance.

BFH built a wooden box to screw onto the pack board's base, which made its empty weight over twenty pounds. In it he carefully packed the stove, food, cooking and eating utensils, and the bivouac equipment. Above the box rested my full climbing pack, foam ground pad, and rolled sleeping bag. BFH would help me shoulder the contraption, which now topped fifty pounds, and adjust the tump line on my head. After that he'd throw a couple of coiled climbing ropes over the top of the pack board, pat me on the shoulder, and say, "OK, George, hit the trail." I think dad was trying to demonstrate to others that his son was tough and had "arrived" as a full-fledged mountaineer. It was his way of expressing that he was proud of me. It may not have impressed others, but it left a lasting impression on me.

The box at the bottom of the pack board was too wide and made turning of the torso and back unwieldy. So I would tension the tump line with my head and hike to base camp with the beast on my back. BFH's custom pack board yielded two salient results: the climb the next day was made easy in comparison, and when I later carried a Kelty frame pack, I truly appreciated its sublime comfort. Climbing with BFH begat such appreciations. They gave me perspective.

One day in the mid-1960s, we were preparing for a climb of Mount Adams. BFH and I were in the basement pulling gear together.

"Hey, Dad, where's the pack board?"

"I burned it." BFH's eyes were sad.

"You did the right thing, Dad," I said. "I know you built and carried that thing in the old days, and it meant a lot to you. But it was a bugger to carry."

BFH nodded, reached around the corner of the work bench and pulled out a new Kelty pack.

"Wow, it's beautiful!" I said.

"It's yours," BFH said.

"Thanks Dad!" I slipped my shoulders through the deeply padded shoulder straps. It felt like a feather.

"You're welcome." BFH tossed me the old Primus stove. "Put that in there," he said, as if to indicate that not all of his nostalgic climbing past was to be discarded. At least not today—not all at once.

Part Two

# High Camp

## 23 A New Guide

*The chance to go my own way.*

I was outside mowing the lawn when dad walked out.

"I just got a call from Jack Melill up at the Rainier Guide Service. He needs another guide. He wants to hire you."

"Sure!" I exclaimed. "When?"

"He wants you up at Paradise tomorrow."

This was my break—the chance to do what I loved doing and to be where I wanted to be—out of an unhappy house. During my own seminar up at Rainier earlier that summer, I had talked with guide Gary Ullin about keeping me in mind for a job. He had just looked at me carefully, nodded, and said "OK, George, I will." Nothing more was said, and now down at home I had quickly pushed the pipe dream to the back of my mind as a long shot, a mere possibility among the greater probabilities for a kid my age in Shelton—a summer job in the woods trimming Christmas trees or logging—or if I was lucky, working at a local restaurant, golf course, or a marina on Hood Canal, where there were chances for tips on top of a paltry salary. Being young I was "entry level" at everything, and I knew it. Everything except climbing. Was I good enough to work up at the Rainier Guide Service? Yes, I thought. I'd been up Mount Rainier four times already, had led the party on two of those climbs run by BFH, and had seen the guides hands-on in the seminar I attended. Heck yes, I could do it. I left the lawn half-mowed and started packing.

Dad drove me up to Rainier from Shelton early the next morning. I could tell he was proud. I was ecstatic.

"Look, George," he said. "Guiding is significantly different from climbing. The clients you take up will have almost no experience. You are only seventeen. Older clients will try to push you around. They may not trust you. You will have to learn how to lead them. Be understanding and patient, but be firm. If you do that they'll come around."

"I understand, Dad," I said. "You've trained me from the beginning as a guide. Your philosophy has always been to immerse new people in mountaineering, and when I grew up in the sport, you had me train them—guide them—just like you do. That's why Gary Ullin was interested in me, I think. It wasn't for any great ability as a climber, but because he saw me during my seminar as a client how I worked with people. That's guiding." I surprised myself with the clarity of my words.

BFH was quiet for a moment, and then said, "Yes, George, it is. Climbers with great ability are a dime a dozen. Good guides are much more rare."

I unloaded my gear at the Paradise Henry M. Jackson Visitor's Center, and dragged it into the RGS facility on the first floor.

"Good to have you on board, George." Jack Melill shook my hand and handed me a guide sweater. It was navy blue wool, with thin white and red pin stripes running horizontally across the chest. It was the sweater of the 1964 French Winter Olympic Team. "Stow your gear on a bunk in one of the rooms across the hall. That's the guide's quarters when they're not on the hill."

"Mr. Melill, when do I start taking trips?"

"In about two hours," he said. "And call me Jack."

Gary Ullin walked in and told me that I would be working a five-day climbing seminar with him. "After a seminar you get two days off," he said, adding, "If you do a regular two-day summit climb, you only get one day off. Gear up and we'll be off." I left my "civilian" clothes and accessories in the gray wooden U.S. Navy locker dad gave me, put on climbing clothes, and reported back to the office. Dad and I shook hands.

"I'll be back next weekend to see how you did, George," he said with a nod, and left to go back down the hill to Shelton.

I had longed for this day—when I could get out of the house and work up at Rainier. Now the day was here, and I was standing on my own feet. A spark of insecurity played among the butterflies in my stomach. I had just graduated from High School, and was scheduled to enter my freshman year at the University of Puget Sound in the fall. But now the sun shone brightly at Paradise this summer day, and I was a guide. I took a deep breath and walked back to the RGS office to help Gary Ullin.

"George, check on that client over there against the wall. He's got his gear all laid out." He handed me a clipboard with an equipment checklist and a list of the clients signed up for the seminar.

"If he's good, he can pack his stuff."

All of the equipment was accounted for. I checked off the client's name on the list.

"Dave, your gear is all here. Good. Go ahead and put it back in you pack," I said. I did that for six more clients, working my way around the crowded room. Gary had completed his group. We were ready to go.

Ullin led the clients down the steps of the Visitor's Center into the bright sunshine. He proceeded to show them how to carry the ice axe safely, "pick backward, thumb under the adz." We swung onto the trail toward Camp Muir. There were 16 clients and two guides. The seminar curriculum was fresh in my memory, as I had just completed one myself as a client a few weeks before.

## *AVOIDING THE SUDDEN STOP*

We hiked off toward the training and practice area. It was a couple of easy miles away, a large snowfield with a vertical lip, or cirque, at its top. Gary trusted me with instructing from the start. He broke the clients into two groups, and I took one of them. Until mid-afternoon we taught the seminar clients how to walk and climb on snow, traversing, knot tying, roped glacier travel, and the self-arrest, done with the ice axe to stop a fall and avoid sudden stops. These clients were in good shape, athletic, and were fast learners.

"OK, George, let's round 'em up and head to Camp Muir," Ullin said. He had me lead. As he directed, I took short steps and just ambled along at a slow pace using the rest step. "You can only go as fast as your slowest client," Gary said, "and the steps you kick must be for the smallest person. Otherwise someone is going to get worn out quickly." The idea was to walk slowly using the rest step, and to minimize rest stops. Ullin walked to the side of the line, correcting a hold on an ice axe here and adjusting a pack for proper fit there.

"Jack, you're scrambling. Relax, do the rest step. Take deep breaths and blow them out. Concentrate on that. Trust your boots. They're built for the snow. Place your boot once and step up on it. If you pick your feet up and re-kick your step all the time you will wear yourself out." The client behind me was a natural for the climb. He had mastered the rest step, so I told him to lead: "Just follow the big trail of tracks to Muir, Barry," I said. In chatting with him I'd found out that Barry was a career Marine who had just returned from a combat tour in Vietnam. He'd seen Mount Rainier from the plane as he arrived back stateside at Sea-Tac international Airport in Seattle, and decided on a whim to take the seminar and climb the mountain. I slipped out to the side to help Gary observe the clients.

"Good, George," Gary said. "Thanks for helping. And you identified the strongest client and tasked him. That's exactly your job—to assess clients' capabilities and then assign them positions and responsibilities accordingly."

"By the way," Ullin said, "Jim Whittaker is coming up to teach the seminar tomorrow." Jim, the first American to summit Mount Everest in 1963, was a mountaineering icon. I pinched myself. Yesterday I was mowing the lawn in Shelton and today I'm up on the "Hill." It was like being called up to the big leagues. Then a strange thought flashed: I guess dad was going to have to finish mowing the lawn.

As we plodded upward, the dark rock huts at Muir, nestled between Muir Peak and the Cowlitz Cleaver, rose distinctly into view. At 10,068 feet, Camp Muir, and the altitude, embraced me like an old friend.

"Leave your pack outside the Guide Hut," Gary said. He ushered me in. "George, this fine lady is named Jill. She is our cabin girl, and she works wonders with crappy food," Ullin quipped.

"Welcome, George, throw your stuff on the top bunk

over there," she said. I've got hot tea ready for the clients, and we'll feed them dinner in about an hour." The burners of the propane stove she stood next to threw steady blue flames around the bottoms of two gigantic aluminum pots. Steam rose above them, wafting a delicious smell my way. "Chicken and rice," she said with a smile.

Gary and I sat out on the steps of the hut after dinner. I had my socks off and was lancing two large blisters, one on each foot.

"New boots," I said. Ullin looked at my feet over his steaming cup of coffee.

"Yeah, it's a pain breaking in new boots. But by the end of this week they should be softened up nicely. Spending all day in the snow with them gets them pliable." He was right.

The second day of the seminar we spent the morning doing more self-arrest practice, first individually, then by rope teams. In the afternoon we swung onto the Cowlitz Glacier for glacier travel.

"Your buddy has just rounded the end of the crevasse ahead of you Joe, and is

Figure 1 Jim Wittaker at Camp Muir, RGS seminar, 1966. Old Mount Saint Helens is on the horizon.

cutting back the other way to round the next one. You have to speed up to make the corner, or your rope will come tight before you get to it," Ullin would say. Gradually, with our coaching, the clients got the knack of rope team travel. They learned how to handle the gold line ropes: when to coil in and let coils out when transitioning from snow to rock and back again, and to keep the slack out of the rope when moving.

Late in the afternoon Jim Whittaker came slogging up the Muir snowfield into camp. It was only three years after his Everest ascent, and he quickly had the clients, and me, mesmerized with his stories. His objective, however, was to impart his learning about judgment in the mountains.

"There are times to push, and times to turn around," Jim said. "The problem with Everest was that we had come halfway around the world with an expedition funded by many interests, from science and medical, to mountaineering equipment manufacturers. It put a lot on our shoulders. When Jake Breitenbach was killed in the first few days in the Khumbu Icefall, we thought about turning around, but we didn't. We pushed on for Jake. Was that the right thing to do? It seems so, after the fact, after we were successful, albeit several came back to lose toes from frostbite—and marriages. So, was it worth it?" Jim let the questions hang in the thin air. The only sound was the hissing of the Coleman lantern. There was distance, almost sadness, in his eyes. He went on.

## AVOIDING THE SUDDEN STOP

"Mount Rainier has all the same risks and challenges of Everest, except for the extreme altitude," he said. "That's why the American Everest team trained up here before going to Nepal. You are subjected to the same risks—cold, wind, icefall, rockfall, seracs, and crevasses—the same as on Everest. As a climber you must balance these risks. All of you want to be successful on a climb or you wouldn't be here. But you must temper your desire for making a summit with the realities and risks at stake. Gaining that balance, that perspective, is something you must seriously strive for right now, at the beginning, and all throughout your mountaineering endeavors. And wherever you are, unless you are climbing solo, you must measure, watch, and look out for, not only yourselves, but all on your rope team, and all in your party. If you do that you will have a decent chance at walking away from the sport at the end and dying in bed." I glanced at the clients' faces. They encircled Jim, illuminated and frozen, like actor's masks, in the light of the lantern on the table next to him. I hoped that some of what Whittaker said was sinking in. The faces were serious, contemplative. They couldn't have heard the words from a better source. Nor could I.

The third day Whittaker, Ullin, and I spent the morning teaching clients rappelling, and in the afternoon we trekked out on the Cowlitz Glacier for crevasse rescue training and instruction on steep snow and ice climbing. When we walked off the glacier to the Muir huts, Jim Whittaker said goodbye and headed down to

Paradise. His celebrity gleaned from being the first American to climb Everest brought with it a full calendar of commitments, both in his public and private life. I knew that he was one of the "several" 1963 Everest expedition members he'd talked about the night before who returned to a dissolute marriage that ended in divorce. I reflected on his comment the night before about relationships. It had surprised me and pressed a button in my own life. Jim Whittaker had gone to Everest, had the good skill and fortune to come back alive, and yet that experience was either the brick or feather which broke his relationship with his wife forever. I was up here because I loved climbing and hated the dissonance in my parents' marriage. Jim was up on Everest because he loved climbing, and yet he retreated from—or avoided—a relationship. I was struck by the emotional similarities between what Whittaker expressed in delicate terms last night, and my own with my family. Clearly, his retreat into the mountains didn't work to solve his domestic predicament. Indeed, if I read him right, it made it worse. And then his questions—"Was it the right thing to do—was it worth it?" It began to dawn on me that the mountains were not meant to be permanent sanctuaries, places to supplant emotional pain with physical, but as experience-aids to understand, and to cope with, life and the human condition in "the flatlands."

"George, have your clients coil up their ropes below the guide hut and queue up for snacks and lemonade,"

## AVOIDING THE SUDDEN STOP

Ullin said, as he unbuckled his crampons, banged them together to knock the snow and crud off of them, and disappeared into the hut. It was late afternoon, and a light reddish haze hung low on the southern horizon, levitating Mount Adams and Saint Helens. Forest fires, I thought.

The fourth Day dawned clear. As we roped up to trek back out onto the glacier, there was a thunderous distant "Crack!" A huge rock collapsed downward from Gibraltar's upper face, spinning, because of its size and distance from us, as if in slow motion. It, and the countless others it dislodged on its descent, splashed fountains of snow on the Cowlitz fifteen-hundred feet below, and cartwheeled crazily a quarter mile before disappearing into the maw of a big crevasse.

"There's the bell for our work shift!" Ullin said to the clients. Some laughed nervously. "But we'll stay away from that bowling alley way over there, OK?" Today, clients carried extra climbing hardware—nylon slings, carabiners, ice screws, and "coat hangers." Ice screws were about ten inches long, hollow, with a screw tip at the business end, and a "D" shaped ring handle meant to clip carabiners into. As the ice screw was turned into a surface, ice would extrude through the open back end of the screw. The theory was that this facilitated faster freezing, creating a stronger, more solid anchor. The coat hangers were ice screws as well, but solid one-fourth inch steel about six inches long, also with a "D" clip-in and turning handle at the top.

Gary located a crevasse field about three hundred vertical feet below Muir on the Cowlitz Glacier. Here there were several seracs, or ice towers, which would serve nicely to teach vertical and direct aid ice climbing. Direct aid is the use of ice screws or other anchors to hold the weight of a climber, either while climbing up, or rappelling off, steep or vertical snow and ice. To build confidence, we gathered the clients around and demonstrated the strength of the hardware. Standing on flat ground, I screwed in a coat hanger and ice screw side by side into a serac. Gary attached a rope and carabiner to each. He chose the biggest client and told him to try to pull them out. He couldn't. He started adding clients to the experiment. It was a tug-of-war with the ice screws. It took five clients pulling straight out as hard as they could to finally pop the wire coat hanger out of its hold, and eight to dislodge the ice screw. They were impressed. Ullin then roped up to me, took a standing belay position, and directed me to climb the serac, reaching up and placing each ice screw at arm's length above me as I went, then threading a nylon web sling loop, or "runner," into its "D" handle, and attaching a carabiner to the runner, before reaching up, taking tension on the gold line and Ullin's belay for balance, and clipping the climbing rope into the carabiner hanging from the runner. The process was repeated: reach up, place and turn in the ice screw flush into the ice, attach a runner and clip in the climbing rope, until I worked my way to the top of the serac.

"OK, George, let go and dangle free from that top screw." Using his standing belay, he then gently lowered me down to the flat snow amidst the clients.

"All right, folks, that's how each of you will do this. One team member will climb and place the ice screws while his buddy belays him. The belayer will let his teammate down to the ground, then you will reverse roles until all have climbed and belayed. Any questions?" Gary asked. There were none. "All right, let's break up into two-man rope teams. George, you take four teams to that serac over there, and the other four teams will stay with me and practice on this one. We have plenty of hardware, so take what you need."

At noon we took a break to eat sack lunches, then resumed the practice until all the clients had both climbed their serac, and belayed their partner up it. The glacier travel back up to camp at the end of the afternoon was fun. The clients were delighted with their training, and so were Gary and I. They were all acclimatized to the altitude and in good mental and physical shape. As we unroped outside the huts and laid out our climbing ropes for tomorrow's climb, Barry, the strongest of the clients gave me a nudge.

"George, the others and I have a bet going on how old you are," he said. I say you're no older than eighteen. How old are you?"

"Twenty," I lied.

"Damn, I wouldn't have guessed that," Barry said.

I nudged him back, and replied in my best New York

accent, "Yous gotta problem wid dat?"

"Nope, George, not at all!" Barry laughed and slapped me on the back. BFH was right. A young guide will be watched.

Tomorrow was the fifth and last day of the seminar—the summit climb. Barry and the rest of the clients were ready, and so was I.

# 24 THE NIGHT CLIMB

*Something to tell the grandkids.*

Gary Ullin stood at the door of the guide hut at Camp Muir. We had just finished up the fourth day of a climbing seminar, and the next day was summit (graduation) day. Gary looked up toward Gibraltar then turned and looked south down the Muir snowfield toward Paradise and the Tatoosh Range. Beyond the park stood Mount Adams, Mount Saint Helens, and Mount Hood, across the Columbia River in Oregon over a hundred miles away. Deepening shadows of the waning western sun burnished the seracs and crevasses of the Nisqually Glacier. His eye scanned back down the wide climbing trail from Muir, past Anvil Rock and Moon Rocks. Though the path narrowed into a finer line with distance, it remained easily distinguishable as it meandered over Pebble Creek and across shrinking patches of snow at Panorama Point. Below "Pan" the trail reemerged to split both sides of Alta Vista just above Paradise Inn and the parking lot. At the west end of the lot, the dark pancake dome of the newly christened Henry M. Jackson Day Use Building, or "DUB," contrasted with its surroundings like the wrong button on a shirt.

Gary sat down next to me on the guide hut steps, coffee in hand.

"George, this has been an excellent week. The clients have been outstanding on this seminar. I have even enjoyed the beef stew." He smiled and carefully sipped from his steaming tin cup, trying not to burn his lips. "We have a perfect weather forecast for tomorrow." Gary looked over his shoulder at the climbing ropes laid out neatly in parallel next to the clients' tents on the Cowlitz. "It may get hot and soft in the afternoon," he added. "But we're ready."

Figure 2 Gary Ullin on the afternoon before the night climb of Rainier.

"Well, Gary, if we're ready, why don't we go?" I

asked.

He looked at me. "What do you mean?"

"Why don't we just do a night climb? We can leave in about an hour. You know the clients don't sleep much anyway before summit day. I can carry a stove, and when we reach the crater, I'll brew up tea for them. They can get a good several hours of rest up there before the sun comes up and loosens the route."

Ullin's eyes brightened. "Great idea! Let's do it!"

I walked over to each of the clients' tents and broke the news. "What do you all think of doing a night climb?"

"Will we have enough battery life in our headlamps?" a client asked.

"Yes, plenty. We will have a half-moon tonight and it's rising early. You will be amazed at how much light is reflected off the snow just from the moon. At the summit I will treat you all to hot tea. You can tell your grandkids you did a night climb of Rainier and sipped tea on the top."

"I'm all for it. That sounds cool," another client said. "I won't be sleeping here at Muir tonight anyway." I looked around the group. They nodded.

"OK, take forty-five minutes to get your gear together and swing by the guide hut to pick up the bag lunches we've prepared for you. Be out next to your rope-in positions in an hour."

We departed Camp Muir at eight thirty. Alpenglow bathed the mountain. Night settled in gently around us.

We switched on our headlamps. The glacial snow, so soft and sloppy in the heat of the day, was now crisp underfoot, allowing crampons to bight effortlessly with our weight. I was carrying a Bluet gas stove with two extra canisters, extra water, and tea bags. Ullin and I also carried sleeping bags and foam ground pads.

Ullin called a break at the top of Cathedral Gap and another brief one at Cadaver Gap below Gibraltar. The night's breeze was cool, but we made good time. With the exertion, some clients needed to take off their parkas. Gary and I had advised them to "leave Muir chilly," meaning that if they dressed down slightly and started climbing on the cool side, moving only a couple of rope lengths would warm them up to a good comfort level. Otherwise, the party would be slowed down with too many stops to adjust clothing. Frequent stops not only kill valuable time, but also break the cadence of the rest step. No other skill is more important in transporting a climber through distance and altitude than the rest step. It is the singular rhythm and efficiency of this movement that gains a summit on a big mountain.

The party left Cadaver Gap, following the Ingraham Glacier's moonscape toward the Headwall. With headlamps off, and except for the gold line running mysteriously off toward a teammate, the mountain folded in around each of us. Breathe in, rock the leg forward, step, come up on a locked knee, pause, and exhale. Inhale, rock, step, lock, pause, exhale. If done correctly, the rest step is yoga. It balances and relaxes the hips, torso, and shoulders with each stride. Done correctly it may be continued for hours without stopping, even on steep terrain.

I looked up. Ullin had briefly switched on his headlamp to locate a wand and confirm our route. He was on the Headwall.

"Folks, it's steeper in here, but that's OK. You are all doing the rest step very well. See how it saves you energy? Now, on the Headwall here, just take shorter steps. Don't repeatedly kick your boots into the same step. Rely on your crampons. Simply place one foot in front of the other and continue the rest step. Stay relaxed. There's no need to tense up at all."

As the clients gained confidence in their abilities and the training they'd accumulated over the prior four days on the seminar, their relaxation was palpable. Our teams crested the Headwall and eased out above Gibraltar Rock and Camp Comfort at 12,300 feet. As we crossed through a set of huge blue crevasses, I could hear sporadic conversations among the clients. They were enjoying the mountain, the beautiful moonlit night, and each other.

Gary traversed the bergschrund at 13,200 feet on a solid snow bridge, angled slightly to the north, and in a few rope lengths switched on his headlamp again. "I can see the crater rocks. We're in, George!" The last client reached the crater rim at two-thirty. We stepped down into the crater and coiled up the ropes. The bright half-moon cast animated shadows as we shook hands and slapped backs.

"Congratulations!" Ullin announced. "You've summited Mount Rainier. But that is not your graduation from this seminar. Graduating is getting back down." He smiled. "George will carry the stove over to Register Rock. We'll crank it up there and make you some tea. This is a particularly balmy night. If you have the energy, I suggest you walk the crater rim. If not, find a good spot near George and me and sack out. I want all of you back at our ropes and ready to head down by no later than nine o'clock."

Gary and I walked across the crater to Register Rock with some of the clients. I found a flat rock protected by the wind, reached into my Kelty frame pack, and pulled out the Bluet stove, an aluminum cooking pot, and several quarts of water. In minutes the Bluet was singing its blowtorch melody as I dumped a handful of tea bags into the water and closed the lid. Ullin unrolled the sleeping bags and ground pads and beckoned clients to have a seat.

"Just make sure you don't step on them with your crampons. They don't last long when you do that."

They sat. In the moonlight they took on dark shapes like crows perching a wire. Presently the pot boiled and steaming tins of hot tea were handed around. I turned the Bluet down, told the clients to help themselves to more, and trudged the few feet up to Columbia Crest at 14,411 feet, the true summit of Rainier. Liberty Cap, one of Rainier's three main summit peaks, reposed quietly to the northwest, splitting the city lights of Tacoma and Seattle sixty miles away. I scanned the crater rim. Headlamps winked on and off periodically. Some of our clients were walking it, enjoying the mountain and the soft sweeping views of landscapes quietly asleep under a bright moon. I followed them.

An hour later I was back at Register Rock brewing more tea on the Bluet. Clients were dribbling in, fatigue having crept up on them. They laid down on the sleeping bags and ground pads. I noticed Ullin curled up asleep a few yards away and chose my own spot—a small beckoning circle of pebbles or pumice among the rocks. Immediately I was asleep.

"Ow!" I yelled myself awake.

"What's the matter?" Gary's voice carried over in the dark. I switched on my headlamp and looked at the ground. Steam was oozing out.

"Damn. I've been sleeping on a steam vent."

"You need to watch out for them," Ullin observed and nodded back to sleep. I found a cooler place to nap. When I awoke, the eastern sky had lightened. It was five o'clock. I lighted the Bluet stove and heated up another round of tea. Clients were scattered around among the crater rocks, some sleeping singly, others huddled in motionless bunches with our sleeping bags pulled across them.

The sun splashed Columbia Crest at six o'clock and quickly bathed Register Rock. The clients were warmed out of their sleep. They stirred, stood up, and stretched. "Come on over and have another cup of tea," I called.

They came. Gary Ullin sipped his tea and looked around at the gathered group.

"Everyone's here. Good. Did you all get some sleep?" A few nodded. "Some of you look like you're still asleep." He smiled, looking around. "OK, here's the deal. We're on schedule to leave at nine o'clock, so you'll need to migrate across the crater to our assembly point no later than eight thirty. Put on a thin windbreaker. On the way down, the wind usually smacks us a bit at the rim. In the meantime get a bite to eat and some more tea or water. It is ten miles from here to the parking lot, all downhill. Your thighs are going to burn. That is normal. Keep your knees bent and your weight out over your feet. Because we're descending earlier than on a regular climb, the snow will be firm and crusty for at least part of the way. Walk with your boots and crampons flat on the snow like you've been taught. You can't dig your heels in and plunge-step until the snow softens. And another thing—" Gary swept his gaze around the group to press his point "—those in back must keep the slack out of the rope for their teammates in front. If you let slack gather around the man in front of you the rope will trip him. If you fall, yell 'falling' and go into an immediate self-arrest with your ice axe. If you see anyone on your team fall, go into an immediate self-arrest. Any questions? None? OK, George and I will see you on the other side of the crater in a couple of hours."

At nine o'clock we departed. Ullin was bringing up the rear of the party. I was anchoring the first rope team down. As I started off, Gary said, "George, if the Headwall is icy, I want you to anchor yourself at the top of it. I and the teams between us in the party will pass through, using you as a fixed rope and hand-line. When I get to the end of your rope I will set an anchor. Then you leapfrog the group through my fixed rope. We'll do that until we clear the Headwall."

Our party moved steadily down past the bergschrund and around the cluster of crevasses at the top of Gibraltar. The snow was beginning to loosen up but not enough. There were still patches of hard crust. I told my strong lead client to ease carefully down the Headwall. When the rope was fully stretched out, I set a boot-axe belay and waved Ullin down. The balance of the party clanked down the face holding on to our rope. A couple of times I felt a slight tug as clients slipped and stopped themselves with our gold line. Presently a shout came back through the party. "Gary is ready."

My team stepped neatly down, ice axes in the right hand, Ullin's rope in the other. I set one more anchor with my team. My lead climber was off the Headwall. I yelled back to Ullin, and the party leapfrogged through. This was a safe means of moving a party through a steep section without using individual belays, which took a lot of time. Moving rope teams are the best belays.

Taking the lead and leaving me to bring up the rear, Ullin swung back out on the Ingraham Glacier, following the winding route as it skirted the northern cliffs of Gibraltar. It was eleven o'clock. We were back in the bowling alley, exposed to rockfall. *Whap.* A rock hit the snow like a bullet not more than ten feet away. *Whap.* Another hit on the other side of me. I figured they'd freefallen from high above, because I could hear no incoming sound.

"Move!" I needn't have yelled. My exposed rope team sprinted the next thirty yards to less exposed ground. Snow water trickling into Gibraltar's basalt cracks had frozen overnight and expanded in the cracks, breaking and loosening rocks. When warmed by the morning sun, the ice melted, creating rockfall. This was its relentless cycle.

The trek back to Camp Muir down through the scree of Cathedral Gap and across the Cowlitz Glacier was a long one. Not in actual time. That was only an hour or so. But in mental distance it was a marathon for clients. The Muir huts, and the end of the technical climb, could now be seen. They seemed tantalizingly near. On hot days, as this was now becoming, the concavity of the Cowlitz Glacier acts like a solar oven. Trudging across it stifles the breath and saps the last strength from stumbling legs. Today, however, our stellar seminar clients showed they had reserve energy.

"Gary, you and George go to the guide hut," client Gordon Hunter said. "We'll coil in the ropes and bring them up to you. That's the least we can do."

By three o'clock that afternoon, our party was off the mountain and in the parking lot at Paradise. We iced the cake that day with a steak dinner down at the Gateway Inn just outside the Nisqually entrance to the park.

After Gary Ullin had handed out the graduation certificates, one of the clients rose for a toast. "Here's to drinking tea on the top, and here's to an amazing night climb!"

"Here, here!"

# 25   THE HUT

*Counting the grains and chasing propane.*

When I joined the RGS in 1966, there were only seven full-time guides—eight counting the owner and manager, Jack Melill. Manager Jack required the guide hut to be manned full time. Since I was the newest and youngest guide, I was tapped. Often I "held down the fort" for a week or more. When RGS parties came up to Camp Muir on the first day of the summit climb, I would join the party, climb the mountain, and stay at the guide hut as the other guides escorted the clients back down to Paradise.

The guide hut was built fifty years before in 1916. Perched precariously on the Cowlitz Cleaver, abutting the edge of the Cowlitz Glacier, crafted from surrounding stone and held together by cement packed in by horse trains, the hut was about fifteen feet wide and thirty long. The nearly flat roof was tarred and supported by strong wooden timbers, to hold up to the deep snow loads of winter. They could be immense. A world record snow depth was recorded down at Paradise in the winter of 1971-72. It totaled ninety three and a half feet. A small window a foot or two square provided the only clue of daylight and a view outside. The heavy wood Dutch door was the only entry and exit, and when guides were out on a climb it would be padlocked shut. Anyone who lost the key had to wash the dishes and fill the water tank. Metal bunk beds and cabinets lined and stacked the walls, and there was a small alcove at the back for storage of climbing gear and supplies.

I loved my solo stays at Camp Muir. Many weekdays saw no climbs or visitors at all, especially in bad weather. My job, along with being the watchman, was to keep the fifty gallon water tank on the hut's roof shoveled full of clean snow. The tank was rectangular and painted black. The sun would melt the contents into fresh water which was fed via pipe and spigot into the cabin. That exercise alone, at 10,000 feet, kept me in good shape. The views were spectacular. It was here in the solitude that the pulse of the Mountain could be felt, and where I could feel mine in it.

The hut, and my bunk with it, shuddered in the force of the wind. It was cold. I had stuffed one sleeping bag inside another and climbed in, but I was still cold. I tried to keep my teeth from chattering as I turned to look out the tiny window. I had chosen the "window bunk," because up here I held seniority—I was alone. The light, so silky in the sunset, had faded pale.

The wind had struck unexpectedly an hour before when I was outside sitting on the steps. Even though I was slightly in its lee, it hit me between the shoulder blades like a hammer, knocking me off balance. Putting a hand down to steady myself, I turned and retreated into the hut, shutting and tying off the Dutch door with the thin nylon cord for that purpose. There was no handle or latch, and only a hasp and padlock anchor on the outside. I lit a match and it fluttered out. I lit another, cupping the flame with my hand, and held it under the mantle of the Coleman Lantern. I turned the pressure valve and with a "pop" the mantle caught the fire, and glowed slowly into a hissing bright light. I slid the glass globe down, grabbed the wire top-handle, and turned around. The white arc of the light caused the rough rock walls to shadow dance. Dust and rock particles swirled around the inside of the hut. They stung the face like hard driven snow, and had been propelled through the concrete seams and cracks of walls built long ago, and yet still stood. With the dust came an intensely cold draft. It was mid-evening and still light outside, but that was rapidly waning in the wind's onslaught. Since the temperature was plummeting there was nothing for it but to climb into a sleeping bag. The noise increased to a roar. I laid there and watched the dark brown wooden ceiling. I traced the grain of the four inch thick boards along their length, past occasional knots. I counted twenty six in one board's width. The next board had the same. The next, nineteen. Does that mean they were that old when they were cut? Not likely. That was 1916, when a lot of the timber was still virgin and hundreds of years old. When the mill's saw sliced a log lengthwise it showed the grain, not the rings that tell the tree's age. I breathed a little more relaxed, even though as I watched, I could see the boards flex slightly in the blasts of wind. My mind shifted outside. Big rocks were cemented together around the edge of the roof where it met the walls to hold it down. Were they big enough? Not tonight. In an hour I had wearied of being worried, and the roaring wind shouted me into a numbed fitful sleep.

I awoke to daylight suffusing the hut. The wind had calmed, and all I could hear was the occasional light skittering of a mouse over paper or cardboard. The contrast between the howling winds last night and their cessation in the morning heightened my sensitivity to their sounds. The guide hut also sported a large pack rat which I named Packy. He was a good tenant, stayed out of the way, and was unobtrusive. I wondered how he fared in the storm—routine for him I thought. I laid there, warm in my dual sleeping bags, and glanced at my watch. It was seven thirty in the morning. The next summit party of clients was not due until three o'clock,

## AVOIDING THE SUDDEN STOP

the roof water tank was full, and I was ahead on all my housekeeping, so I rolled over and went back to sleep. I awoke a couple of hours later to the sounds of voices outside. I bailed out on my sleeping bags and swung out the top Dutch door. Two hikers, a man and woman, sitting on the guide hut steps jumped up, startled.

"We didn't know anyone was here," the lady said.

"That's OK. Go ahead and sit back down and enjoy the view," I said. They introduced themselves:

"I'm Thomas, the man said, and this is Gretchen." Both were tan and lean. Gretchen was also blond and well-proportioned.

"I'll be with you in a minute," I said. I slipped my wool knickers over my long johns, lighted the propane stove and put a small pot of water on it to boil, then joined the couple outside. We shook hands.

"How was your trip up to Muir?"

"Wonderful! " Gretchen said, in a slight German accent. "We left Paradise this morning after the wind died down."

"What time was that?"

"Oh, maybe four thirty?" she looked at Thomas. He nodded, smiling.

"You made excellent time," I said.

"We did?" she said.

"Yes, three hours is moving right along. Normal hiking time from Paradise to Muir is four to six hours."

"Really?" she said. Thomas and Gretchen talked in German, and nodded.

"Such times must be considering carrying heavy loads for climbing, yes?"

"Yes," I said. "Would you two like a cup of coffee?"

I brought out two steaming cups. Looking down toward Pebble Creek I could see a long line of black specks just clearing the crest of Panorama Point. This was the RGS party en route for tomorrow's summit attempt. I found out that Thomas and Gretchen were Austrians from Salzburg. They were taking the summer off to drive around the U.S.A. They asked about the routes above Muir, and said that next year they may be back to give the summit a try. An hour later Thomas and Gretchen walked back down the Muir Snowfield. They moved swiftly, and presently their forms, now miniaturized by distance, disappeared into the swale below Anvil Rock. I stood up, and went to shovel more snow into the water tank, and prepare the camp for the incoming clients. "What a job!" I said to myself, "I've got the best view in the western states, I get to meet folks from all over the world, climb Mount Rainier, and get paid for it!"

The guide hut at Camp Muir required constant resupply of food and equipment. On a trip up the mountain with clients, guides usually carried forty to sixty pounds of these items in addition to their own gear. Such sundries as cans of beef stew, jars of peanut butter, jam, bags of oatmeal, rice, and bread, were common additions to our packs. But several times over the summer season airdrops were required. Grill-sized propane canisters were needed to run our stoves in the guide hut to feed the hundreds of clients that paid for seminars or summit climbs. Jimmy Beech flew these missions for decades.

"Jimmy is going to drop propane up there this afternoon." Guide service owner Jack Melill's voice crackled over the old Motorola radio at Camp Muir.

"OK, Jack," I said. "We'll be looking for him." Jack Hebert and I were staffing Muir for the week. Weather was clear and the air was still. Nevermore, our resident raven, was contentedly lounging on Muir Peak, just east of the public hut. He boded perfect conditions for an airdrop. The big bird was a barometer. He flew to lower ground when he sensed impending bad weather.

"I see him," Jack called in. I stepped out of the guide hut and looked south down the long Muir snowfield toward Paradise and the Tatoosh Range beyond. A small white speck was droning, gradually building altitude. It was Jimmy's trusty old Cessna 185, the same one I had taken my first flight in years ago. It flew with methodical authority, turning in great climbing circles as it slowly worked its way in our direction.

Muir Peak forms the southeastern pommel of the rock saddle that separates the Muir snowfield from the Cowlitz Glacier. Camp Muir nestles in that saddle. Jimmy's first pass was a test run to gauge the wind. A large white wing flashed east to west just south of Muir Peak and waggled at us. The Cessna's passenger door was off, and a guide's hand waved to us as Jimmy coasted out over the Nisqually Glacier and banked hard left, circling around for the drop.

Figure 3 Bush Pilot Jimmy Beach prepares for an RGS airdrop of supplies at Camp Muir. The Tatoosh Range is below and Mount Adams is on the horizon.

"OK, Jack, get ready. He's making his drop pass next."

Jimmy disappeared to the east, and there were a few moments of silence. Then suddenly his plane appeared, made a hard left turn over the Cowlitz near Cathedral Rocks, and headed straight for us. As he bored in, he cut his engine, side-slipped hard to the right, dropped his right wing, and out plummeted two propane canisters. The plane's wheels were no more than twenty feet off the ground. The canisters sent up splashes of spray as they hit the Muir snowfield and began to tumble. Jack started to run after them, but I grabbed him.

"He's going to make another drop, Jack. You don't want to be in the way of it." Back Jimmy came again, deftly threading the needle. A sideslip, a dipped wing, and out came three more tanks. Two hit the snow, but one hit the rocks near camp and exploded in a fireball.

"Wow!" Hebert's face reflected glee at the fireworks, and Jimmy waggled his wings again as he skimmed away, signifying that the drop was over. We ran off down the Muir snowfield, chasing propane tanks. Some had bounced and rolled more than a thousand feet. By the time Jack and I had retrieved them we were sweating and panting. Collecting airdropped supplies was always a workout, but with Jimmy Beech, it was always a thrill—and a godsend.

As Jack and I sat on the steps of the guide hut after our propane workout, I thought back to my first flight, and that is was with Jimmy. It was almost a decade since that grand initiation to flying, capped with a winged tour of The Mountain. In some ways Jimmy Beech had the best of both worlds—he was experienced enough to get close in and fly the nooks and crannies of Rainier—and yet to get there he didn't have to fight the cold, crevasses, ice and rockfall. And he slept in a warm bed at night.

## 26  A Pack Rat's Tale

*"And thereby hangs a tale." –Shakespeare*

A stay at the guide or public huts at Camp Muir was sure to bring any visitor into contact with the huts' permanent residents—rats and mice. Muir was built, and for many years resupplied, by pack trains of horses or mules. In the mid-1960s this was no longer done, but by this time many generations of the furry creatures had not only survived but thrived. To thrive is to multiply.

Guides and cabin assistants who resided for days at Muir were inexorably immersed in experiences with the furry little creatures. We would set traps. One night I caught six mice. I would just clear out the trap, reset it, turn out the light, and snap!

Mice could easily hitch rides up to Camp Muir in climbers' packs. Rats were another matter. Being much larger, they obtained their rides up to camp on pack animals. The one and only type of rat I encountered in the guide hut was the pack rat. "Packy" was a medium-sized rat with shiny brown fur, long whiskers, and a long naked tail with a bottle brush on the end. He never bothered anyone, other than keeping boarders awake. After putting the light out at night, I could count to about thirty in my sleeping bag before Packy started his shift. He was a proper, well-mannered, and discreet creature. He never made loud noises. In the light of the next morning, if a bunk bed was moved, I would inevitably find one of Packy's stashes tucked back in a niche or corner of the old rock hut. A sliver of red surveyor's tape from a wand, a scrap of an oatmeal box, a shoelace. All such bobbles were fair game and fondly gathered. One day, however, Packy abused his discretion.

In the first week of June of 1967, as the RGS ramped up its summer season with a post winter cleanup of the guide hut, owner Jack Melill sent us up to build rock foundations for two big army tents that would house our clients. These foundations became those for the permanent Rainier Mountaineering Inc. (RMI) client huts that grace Camp Muir to this day.

Jay Ullin, Jim Ullin, Jay Sprenger, Jack Hebert, Don McPherson, and I were among the work contingent. We made good progress. Rocks were hauled, a foundation wall was built, and gravel and dirt were shoveled into the middle and compacted. We had worked hard, the day was hot, and we were all drenched in sweat. We returned to the guide hut, had dinner, and prepared for bed. The bunks were all taken, so Jay Sprenger threw his foam sleeping pad on the floor of the hut and crawled into his bag. There was much lying and bragging going on and a little celebratory drinking. At eleven o'clock we shut down the Coleman lamp and settled down to sleep. The air was cold; the hut was pitch-dark. Perfect for a good night's sleep.

"Aaahhhh!" A scream rent the silence. It was Jay Sprenger. I sat up and hit my head on the bunk above. We switched on our headlamps.

"What the hell happened, Jay? Are you OK?" Jim asked.

"No! I just got licked!"

"Licked? By what?"

"That damned pack rat."

"Where did he lick you?"

"Right on the side of my face." Sprenger's eyes were wide as he pointed to his cheek.

"How did you know it was the pack rat?"

"Because," Jay retorted, "he had a big slimy tongue, and I could feel his long whiskers!"

The reason for Packy's move was logical. Sprenger's sweat from the day's work had dried on his face. Jay was just a big salt lick to Packy.

"Well," Jim mused, "at least you knew it wasn't one of us. We don't have our beards grown out yet."

Jay didn't see the humor. "I'm serious. I will not sleep down on this floor until we find that damned thing."

The underwear brigade sprang into action. We donned headlamps, grabbed ice axes, and bent down peeking into corners. Our lights revealed a few cracks as well.

"There he is!" Hebert's voice was shrill. He took a swing with his axe, barely missing Jim Ullin's head.

"Damn, missed. I think he darted behind that cabinet." Jay Ullin was on the top bunk judiciously acting as spotter and directing operations. McPherson made a jab with his axe behind the cabinet as we tilted it forward. The shaft ricocheted off the wall and banged Jim in the head. Six guides flailing away with sharp weapons in the confines of the guide hut was like having a sword fight in a phone booth. Things were getting out of hand. Jim, now twice menaced, but still game for a fight, put on his rock helmet.

Jay Ullin spoke from the upper bunk. "We're going about this all wrong," he said. "What we need to do is open the Dutch door, and when the rat makes a break for it, we nail him. Sprenger, squeeze up against the stove. Hebert, get over across from Sprenger. Don, you and George put your axes down, go to the back of the hut and slowly start pulling bunks and boxes out from the walls. It should drive the rat toward the door."

That sounded like a plan. Slowly, Don inched out the bunks on his side of the hut. Nothing. Slowly I inched out the bunk on my side. My headlamp caught a flitting shadow.

"There he is!" I shouted. Don jumped over to my side

and yanked out a box of beef stew stored against the wall beyond my bunk. Out streaked Packy, headed for the open hut door. Sprenger took a mighty swing with the adz of his axe, sparks flew as the head clanked off of the stone floor.

"I got him!" Sprenger cried. We shined our headlamps toward the door. Inside, next to the threshold, was a small pool of blood, but no rat. We looked closer. Laying a few inches away was half of a rat's tail. It was the bushy end.

Somewhere out in the dark night at Camp Muir, Packy had escaped and was nursing the bloody stump of a bobbed tail. The excitement of the hunt subsided. Sprenger slammed the hut door, and we all eventually drifted off to sleep. But I couldn't help feeling sorry for Packy.

In the weeks after, when I manned Muir all alone, I would occasionally see Packy, back at home in the guide hut, and feed him an extra raisin or peanut. His tail was squat now, but he was a wise and mellow fellow. He forgave the bewildering assaults on him back on that harrowing night in early summer by men in underwear wielding axes, but he could not forget, because he had his stub to remind him. And thereby ends a tail.

## 27 THE WORK

*Once a guide always a guide.*

As I've related, my father launched my mountain journeys earlier than most; but his experiences started young as well. BFH is aptly described by Dee Molenaar in his book *The Challenge of Rainier* (1970) as a "vintage climber." BFH started climbing when he was sixteen, during the height of the Great Depression, when his father told him to go out and find a job because he couldn't afford to feed him. From his home in Tacoma, Washington, my father migrated up to Mount Rainier, circa 1930. It was a natural choice during hard times. Throughout BFH's childhood, his parents, Ben and Slava Heuston, spent most of their free and vacation time camping and hiking in the park.

BFH worked nine summers and two winters in the

Mount Rainier National Park. He managed the now-defunct hotel cabins at Paradise, and in his free time he guided with Frank "Swede" Willard, the chief guide for the RGS. There he gained his experience. He kept his green wool guiding shirt and handed it down to me, which I in turn wore when I worked at RGS, along with the more contemporary blue wool sweater issued during my tenure in the '60s.

One foggy summer afternoon in 1967, I was leading a group of clients back from a tour of the ice caves. Out of the mist walked the noted guide and climber Dee Molenaar with one of his kids in tow. He stopped me and asked, "Are you with the guide service?"

"Yes," I said.

"Where did you get that green shirt?"

"It was the old guide shirt handed down to me from my dad, Frank Heuston."

"Well, I'll be darned," Dee said. "When you came at me out of the fog I thought you were a ghost! Tell Frank hello for me."

That was the way it was in the Rainier guiding and climbing community. It was a small, friendly fraternity. BFH never considered himself a full-fledged guide, but he was, and he was well known and accepted by Dee Molenaar and the other RGS employees of that era.

At bottom, guiding is simple. It is shepherding. The shepherd-guide's job is to anticipate, to know the route, the weather, and the mountain, to think for his clients, to put himself in their shoes, and while they are in his

## AVOIDING THE SUDDEN STOP

care, to know the clients better than they know themselves. Getting a sense of the clientele is a dynamic exercise. Guides gain experience in the profession, and in assessing clients' mental and physical abilities, and use those assessments to determine the makeup of the summit rope teams. Strong, steady clients are the jewels of a guided party. They are placed on the ends of a rope team as anchors or next to weaker clients to bolster them. In the '60s we often guided groups of up to twenty with only two guides. That required choosing strong clients to lead their own teams.

Evaluating clients began at the RGS equipment rental counter, through the one-day preparatory climbing school, and throughout the summit climb itself. At the climbing school, we taught how to safely walk with an ice axe, the rest step, the ice axe self-arrest, knot tying, roped glacier travel, use of crampons, and use of the prusik sling for crevasse rescue. We carefully observed the clients who would leave the next day to head up to Camp Muir for the summit climb: "Bob has two left feet and keeps walking out of his crampons." "Joe's not quick enough on the self-arrest." "Bill looks beat. He's not in shape and scrambles all the time. He's not using the rest step." "Jim is big and strong, but he's muscle-bound. He might wear himself out." "Sam over there is a real trooper. He's in shape, strong, has a great attitude, and watches after others. He's a natural for this climb. We'll use him as a rope leader." And on it went.

Of course, assessments could be wrong. Clients could be harboring fears or physical ailments. They may choose to climb Mount Rainier specifically to test their heart or other conditions but not disclose them as required on their RGS health waiver forms.

As we ascended the mountain on one memorable 1966 summit climb, one of my clients, Jules, began complaining and moving more slowly. Because of this I was out of communication with the guides and their teams above me.

When we finally crossed the bergschrund marking the summit ice cap, Jules stopped. "I can't go on," he exclaimed.

"Jules, you have to continue. It's just a few more rope lengths to the top. The slope eases off. You can do it." We had made it up past Disappointment Cleaver, which was the last safe place we could leave Jules in a sleeping bag to be picked up on our return.

"No!" Jules sat down.

"Get up and walk."

"No, I won't."

"You have to get up and walk." I leaned hard on his rope. He got up, took a dozen more steps, and sat down again. "Jules, get up."

"No. I want to stay here. Go on without me."

"I can't do that. It's too exposed here. We passed the point of no return back at the cleaver. If you were feeling unwell, why didn't you speak up then? We could have left you there." Jules didn't respond. "Get up!"

## AVOIDING THE SUDDEN STOP

"No!"

"Get up, or we're going to pull you up."

"I'm not going!" he shouted. Jules was one of six other clients on my rope. Luckily the others were strong young college students. While Jules sat sullenly, I brought the rest of my team up around me.

"We have a problem here, folks. There are just a couple more rope lengths to the crater rim. We must get there to recontact the rest of the guide party, and I know that all of you have put in a hell of a lot of effort to climb up this far, and you want to summit this mountain." They nodded. A couple of them glanced furtively at Jules sitting in the snow.

"OK, here's the drill," I said. "There are no more crevasses we need to worry about, so we can all cluster together. Coil in and bunch up with me. Leave Jules where he is back there. You folks grab onto the rope and help me. We are going to drag him. Hopefully it will only be a few feet before Jules gets the message, stands up, and walks." The kids nodded, grabbed hold of the rope to Jules, and pulled.

"Stop! I don't want to go!" Jules screamed. He began flailing and even tried to self-arrest to stop us. But up he went, slowly, leaving a furrow in the snow. "You're killing me!"

"No, Jules, we're not killing you. Relax. You would use much less energy if you just stand up and walk and lean back on the rope while we pull you. The top is just up here a few feet."

"No, stop, you're killing me. I'm going to die!"

We dragged him upward. The crater rim was a rope length away. "Stop! You're killing me! I'm going to die!" Jules kept screaming. I had heard enough.

"Jules, if you're going to die, get up on your feet and die like a man." He continued flailing. We dragged him up over the rocks of the rim, and he rolled down in a heap in the shallow crater.

"Well, Jules, with the good graces of your teammates you have made it to the summit of Mount Rainier. Congratulations," I said. Between breathless curses, Jules repeated that I had almost killed him. I leaned down and spoke into his ear. "Not yet, Jules, but don't tempt me. We have the climb down in front of us. I don't know what's eating on you. You seemed fine at the cleaver, then you came apart. You're not that tired, because you had plenty of energy to fight me and the rest of your rope team. In fact you used twice as much effort doing that than if you'd just stood up and walked. You'd better get yourself together while we're resting here," I warned. "Because when we start back, if you sit down and pull a fit on me like that again, I'm going to make your life very miserable, understand?" Jules just glared at me. "So when we go down, stand up, walk, and shut up—like a man."

I crossed the crater to Register Rock and talked to Karl Spahn. "Karl, Jules has flaked out on me. He's claiming I'm going to kill him by making him walk. Can you take him on your rope?"

"I've noticed he's caused you trouble," Karl said. "But you keep him. I'll make sure that we stay closer to you to give you support. Jules was in my climbing school a couple of days ago. He was a big asshole. I told the manager that Jules wasn't suited for the climb, but he told me to take him anyway."

My chat with Jules seemed to work for a while. We arrived at the top of Disappointment Cleaver in normal time. However, as the party worked its way down and off the cleaver and traversed out onto the Ingraham Glacier, Jules began to act up again. He sat down frequently.

"Get up, Jules, we're losing sight of the rest of the party."

"I don't care."

I'd badger him, he'd stand up, walk a few feet, and sit down again. Now every time Jules sat down I leaned hard on his waistband with the rope. He started swearing again. We were almost off the Ingraham Flats and nearing the turn into Cathedral Gap. Good, I thought. Maybe we can get off this mountain before dark. I turned and headed for the gap. The rope moved smoothly. I rounded the corner and stepped onto the scree next to Karl.

"George, where is Jules?" I looked back and my jaw dropped. He had unroped! The rest of my clients were with me.

"Karl, we stopped for him again for the twentieth time just back a couple of hundred yards. Jules finally got up, and I started off. Damn, the team was finally moving. I had no idea that he'd slipped out of the rope, and none of the other clients told me." Karl just sat with me, quietly staring up the trail.

Ten minutes later Jules came sauntering around the corner. He gave Karl and me a wave with his ice axe. It looked more like the finger. Spitting mad, Karl stomped out to him and dragged him to the rocks.

"You are a disgrace to this group! I told them you were no good for this climb, but they made me take you!" Karl's Austrian accent thickened with his anger.

"I don't like George," Jules said.

"Shut up! You don't like anybody but yourself. Get back in the rope!"

"I don't want to get back on George's rope," Jules protested weakly.

"Get back in that rope where you belong or I'm going to bend this around your schtupid head!" Karl waved his axe in Jules's face. "You will climb with George. I will be right next to you, and if you open your mouth again I veel kick your sorry ass! If you sit down I veel pick you up and then I veel kick your sorry ass!"

Jules stammered an "OK" as Karl dragged him roughly back to my rope and cinched the bowline around Jules's waist, making sure it was uncomfortably tight.

We completed our trek back to Camp Muir without another word from Jules. But Karl had plenty to say. Every step of the way across the Cowlitz Glacier, Karl walked next to Jules and shouted in his ear like a Prussian drillmaster. The Austrian philosophy of guiding is simple and direct—you ruin their day and they will ruin yours.

This incident was an aberration, but it had an ironic ending. Six weeks later the RGS received a letter of apology from Jules. He wrote that only a few months before he had undergone heart surgery. He had decided to test his heart condition by signing up for a guided climb of Mount Rainier. He admitted that he hadn't disclosed this on his health waiver form. As he climbed higher on Rainier he first became anxious, then scared, as his heart began skipping occasional beats. He really was terrified that he was going to die, and that his guide, George Heuston, was going to kill him. The letter ended by stating, "Please tell George that I am very sorry for the way I acted toward him and all the rest of the party. I don't know how he and Karl Spahn put up with me. They took me to the top of Mount Rainier and brought me back safely. I shall be forever indebted to them for that. Sincerely, Jules."

It is impossible to plumb all the motivations of clients who seek to climb Rainier. That is part of the territory that comes with guiding. One thing is certain: if there is a physical or mental button concealed by a client, Rainier will push it.

## 28   A Guide's Fare

*"This is your food appreciation course."* –BFH

The RGS paid well. I could pay my way through the next year of college with a summer's wages, but the meal situation up on the hill was another matter. There were no meals included with the job, only a room in The DUB across the hall from the RGS store. We guides had no kitchen facilities, only a hot plate and a sink next to it in the gear drying room. I quickly tired of Kraft macaroni dinners, and food at the DUB cafeteria and at the Paradise Inn was prohibitively expensive. This led to catching our meals on the sly. The first step was to co-opt one of the waitresses or food servers.

"Hey, Sally, can you get me through the line?" Sally worked the cafeteria line in the DUB.

"Sure, wait a minute." Sally scanned the cafeteria for

the manager. He wasn't there. "Come on through."

I would grab a tray, a plate, silverware, roast beef (two helpings), corn, mashed potatoes, peas, beans, tossed salad, Waldorf salad, and two pieces of cherry pie, nod and smile past Sally and the cash register, and be eating back at my bunk in under five minutes.

Sally and the other Park Service employees took good care of us. Slipping guides through the chow line was a game for Sally and her fellow summer workers. But we were not able to avail ourselves of this access often enough. Climbing Rainier burned buckets of calories; I would drop fifteen to twenty pounds in the course of a season, and I routinely dropped ten pounds after each summit trip, regardless of what I ate. Much was loss of water, but I could never consume enough calories to compensate for those burned. Enter Ruth, my mother. She and BFH would drive up to Paradise on the weekends and put on a picnic for me.

When I started up at the RGS I was a picky eater. I was seventeen years old, and I hated ham, broccoli, spinach, cauliflower, watermelon, tossed greens, lima beans, and beef tongue and heart. What did Mom bring to the picnic? All of the above. Did I eat it? I wolfed it down. Nothing corrects a finicky eater like a little starvation.

Mom was brilliant. To this day I love ham, broccoli, spinach, cauliflower, watermelon, and tossed greens. Had I starved a little more, she'd have converted me to lima beans, tongue, and heart. But that's the German in me.

## 29  The Wolfman Wakeup

*A good wakeup alarm gets the blood moving.*

"Hey, girl, what's your name?" The voice of Wolfman Jack welled up on the radio.

"Cindy," replied a wispy teenage voice.

"Why you callin' the Wolfman?"

"My boyfriend left me."

"I'm sorry, Cindy girl. The Wolfman has some special words for ya. Put your ear close to the phone." The Wolfman's voice trailed off to a rasp. "Ya got your ear right up to the phone, Cindy?"

"Yes."

"*Ahhhwoooo!*" The sandpaper whisper into the phone gave way to a wail, followed by the Wolfman slamming down his receiver. He spun up "Lil Red Riding Hood" by Sam the Sham and the Pharaohs.

It was time to get up.

Two hundred and fifty thousand watts of illegal broadcasting power blasted through the transistor radio at the Camp Muir guide hut, transforming it into a boom box. We all shouted as Wolfman Jack spun a song with a driving, pulsating beat. It was twelve thirty on an RGS summit day.

The Wolfman was cranked up to full volume. Clients who couldn't sleep were startled. Clients who slept were jolted awake. I walked out of the guide hut and made the rounds, making sure the clients were complying with reveille. Some complained.

"That's so loud. Who is that?"

"That's Wolfman Jack," I said. "He comes in clear as a bell after dark up here. Isn't he great?"

"Disgusting," a client would say.

"OK, folks, time to rise and shine. Get your summit packs ready and your crampons on. Then come by the guide hut. We'll inspect your crampons and hand you your bag lunches and some hot oatmeal and coffee for breakfast. We want everyone geared up and lined up there by one o'clock." Grumbling usually followed. But the incessant shtick of Wolfman Jack hounded them on.

"Hey, young man, you have a song request for the Wolfman?"

"Yes, I'd like you to play some Elvis songs."

"The Wolfman hears ya, son. Comin' right up!"

"Come on, baby, light my fire," blared out by the Doors. The Wolfman ignored the caller's request. We laughed and put on our own gear. The song ran a full ten minutes, interspersed with the Wolfman crying "*Ahhhwoooo!*" All of us in the hut echoed "*Ahhhwoooo!*"

Wolf howls and rock music drove out vestiges of sleepiness and got the blood moving. The first clients were at the door. Dave Stelling and I inspected crampons, and the cabin girl, Nancy Brown, handed out lunch bags and bowls of steaming oatmeal topped with hydrated powdered milk, cinnamon, and sugar.

"When you're done, grab a cup of coffee," she said.

"Hey, this is the Wolfman coming to you from XERB out of Hollywood, California," Wolfman Jack's washboard vocal cords reverberated. "Two hundred and fifty thousand watts of moon-howlin' rock and roll, baby!"

Station XERB was not in Hollywood. It broadcast across the U.S. border from towers in Rosarita Beach, Mexico. The massive signal beamed up the West Coast, reflected cleanly off Mount Rainier's great bulk, and pounded into our ears at Camp Muir.

Guides and clients took their positions and roped up. "Lead off, George," Stelling called from the end team. As our summit party crumped along over the frozen crust of the Cowlitz Glacier, the sounds and music of Wolfman Jack gradually faded into the folds of the mountain. We started the climb precisely on time: one thirty in the morning. Wolfman Jack kept us on track.

# 30 THE CLIENTS

*Climbing is about mountains in people. Guiding is about people in mountains.*

The clientele of a guide service is a heady mix of those who undertake risk, hardship, and adventure with others they neither know nor trust. Yet, the testament to them is carved in stone—the mountain.

In the three summers I guided on Rainier, in '66, '67, and '68, we failed to summit only once in thirty-four attempts. True, one or two clients on a given trip would tap out for various reasons and be left in designated "safe bivouac" points, such as atop Disappointment Cleaver, to await pickup on the party's return. Most, however, made it up the hill to sign the summit register and cap what for many would be the achievement, and thrill, of a lifetime. A 1967 postclimb survey of clients by the RGS was revealing: over ninety-percent responded that climbing Mount Rainier was the most difficult effort of their lives, both mentally and physically.

The RGS had a philosophy of trying. Despite inclement conditions, including high winds and snowstorms, we would at least rope the clients up and leave high camp; only lightning storms would keep us buttoned up inside the huts. It is surprising how many climbs that departed Muir with what guides gauged to be no better than a twenty percent chance of summiting, were ultimately successful. I especially enjoyed these "challenging" trips because clients gained instant respect for the mountain. Bad weather became the irreducible denominator in welding teams together. Fair-weather clients often completed an entire summit climb without ever becoming a team. Illustrations are in order.

Good days on Rainier brought views of the world that screamed out to be appreciated. I found it frustrating as a guide to see clients on such days focus selfishly inward, squabble, or generally decide to be disagreeable. In 1966 I had a psychiatrist on my rope. He was burly and bad-tempered. He badgered his fellow climbers and railed at all my decisions. We made it to the summit, but it wasn't pleasant for anyone—all because of this one client's tantrums. At Register Rock I pulled lead guide Karl Spahn aside. Karl was only five-foot-seven, but he was all spring steel.

"Karl, something is wrong with this client. He's a shrink, and he's constantly jacking everyone up. Do you

## AVOIDING THE SUDDEN STOP

think he may be playing head games with us?"

"Maybe," Karl said. "If he is, he's making everyone else miserable for the money they've paid to be up here. I'll watch him."

If the climb up was bad, going down was worse. The doctor began swearing at his teammates and berating them. I told him to stop. He ignored me. Then he decided to just sit down on the snow and not move.

"Doc, we just had a rest break, and we need to get down off these glaciers sometime today and before the snow bridges soften up."

"I'll take a break when I want to." The day and the situation were heating up. Every time the doc sat down after that I would lean hard on the rope, making him quite uncomfortable. Finally I rounded the corner to Cathedral Gap and caught up with Karl, who was waiting with the rest of the party. Karl walked past me and grabbed the hapless doctor by the scruff of the neck with an iron grip. He slammed the client up against a rock and raised the shaft of his ice axe up to his face like a giant pointing finger.

"You are a problem! You have been a problem all day!" Doc tried to argue, but that just made Karl angrier. He raised the client completely up off the ground, pack and all, with one hand, and shook him. "Shut up! You have ruined this climb for everyone. You are conducting some kind of psychology experiment, right?"

"Yes," the Doc gasped.

"Well, your bullshit is over, understand?" Without

waiting for an answer, Karl set him roughly down. "And if you don't understand, I will try my own experiment on you with this!" Karl waved his ice axe in front of the doc's now-colorless face. "Now if I hear another word out of you, or if you sit down and slow this party down again, I will kick your ass all the way to Camp Muir." I could see the other clients smiling. The rest of the trip was blissfully uneventful.

In contrast, and as a rule, foul weather brought fair clients.

Dave Stelling and I were on a midweek climb with fifteen clients. Dave was a rangy six feet tall. He guided Rainier in the summer and was a ski instructor at Sun Valley, Idaho, in the winter. We awoke at twelve thirty in the morning to the buffeting of tents and huts.

"What do you think, George?" Dave looked at me after we both poked our heads outside. "Shall we scrub the climb?"

"I'm tempted to, Dave. But we seem to have a strong party. Let's rope them up and take them a ways out on the Cowlitz and see how it goes."

The farther we climbed, the greater the comfort level we gained in coping with the elements. I had prelectured the clients: "Today will be a bit of a challenge, folks. We will not take unnecessary risks out there, but we know the route, it's a good one, and the weather is challenging but not worsening. We will take it as far as prudence permits, OK?" The clients nodded. So off we trekked. We made it across the Cowlitz and up to Cathedral Gap to our first rest stop.

"What do you think George?"

"Dave, these clients are blending well. They're watching out for each other and melding into good teams. I think we can take them at least up to the base of Disappointment Cleaver."

"I agree," Dave said.

At the base of Disappointment Cleaver we stopped briefly. "Dave, what do you think?"

"Let's get them onto the cleaver. If the wind is worse there, we'll turn around."

"Fair enough." The wind on the cleaver was only slightly worse than on the Ingraham Glacier. We worked our way to the top of Disappointment at 12,300 feet. Despite the conditions, we were making good time.

"What do you think? There's a cap on top," Dave noted. Cloud caps form on Rainier with regularity. They can be benign or bode ill.

"Yes, but it's not moving down the mountain, and that's a good sign that our weather, though not comfortable, is at least stable for now," I countered.

"What do you say we take a few more steps?" Dave mused. We topped the bergschrund at 13,200 feet and entered the cap, which was swirling cloud and fine light snow.

"What do think, George?"

"We can still see below us, the wands are all up and holding, so we have a stable, well-marked route."

"Climb a few more rope lengths?" Dave's face, peaking out of the deep fur-rimmed hood of his down parka, smiled through.

"Sure."

As we neared the crater rim, the wind intensified to gusts above fifty miles per hour. Dave and I crawled over the rim rocks, down into the shelter of the crater bowl, and coiled in our clients. There was no question of going over to Register Rock. We would have a bite of lunch and head directly down. It was only ten thirty in the morning, but we knew that this return was going to take more time. As I sat among the crater rocks eating my peanut butter sandwich, I was startled when a chipmunk scampered across my legs. I knew that they were rumored to be up there, subsisting on discarded scraps of food and living in the warm steam caves and vents that affirmed Mount Rainier's identity as a big volcano. I peeled apart half of my sandwich and set it down. It was my offering to the summit's fauna.

"Hey, guys," I yelled through the wind at the gathered clients. "You have done magnificently today, and with your great teamwork we were lucky to summit. Now, I know we're tired. That's normal. But the descent today will require extra concentration. The light snow we're getting is going to ball up under our crampons, and the likelihood of falling is elevated. I want you to all make sure that you keep slack out of the rope to your partners. If anyone slips, yell 'Falling!' like you were taught, and everyone goes immediately into a self-arrest,

OK?" Dave and I looked into the serious faces and knew they got the message. "All right, let's blow this cave!"

Falls began almost at once. Soft new snow balled up under crampons, and slips resulted from loss of footing. At first the clients lay prone on the snow for several minutes with ice axes dug in under them in self-arrest positions. But as we moved along, and they gained confidence in their abilities, Stelling and I observed clients morphing swiftly into mountaineers. When we arrived back at Disappointment Cleaver, they were veterans. By the time we slogged and stumbled back to Muir, I reckoned we'd had more than twenty arrested falls. But by then the rope teams popped quickly back up from their self-arrests and pressed right along without a word. It buttressed the old guiding maxim that "a moving rope team is the best belay."

We were now a band of brothers. Dave and I were profuse in our compliments on this day. The clients swelled with satisfaction and pride at their summiting of the mountain and of overcoming palpable adversity. We were proud of them. This was one of the best climbs I ever had of Mount Rainier.

Guiding and climbing Rainier was not always about the views and good weather. It was about mental discipline and building confidence in oneself and others.

During the 1960s Rainier guides had a policy of separating girlfriends from boyfriends and spouses from each other. They would be placed on different rope teams and as far apart in the party as we could get them.

Several times the man would crap out, we would put him in a sleeping-bag bivouac at the top of Disappointment Cleaver, and his girlfriend or spouse would have no idea that he'd been cut out of the party until the group reached the summit.

"Where's my husband, Carl?" a wife would say.

"Oh, he was having difficulties, so we left him back on the cleaver. He wasn't feeling well." Though sometimes anger would follow surprise, it still meant that at least one of the couple summited. It was our experience that if the man dropped out and the woman knew about it, she would want to quit as well to salve his ego, even though she remained fully capable of making it to the top.

In this respect, and at the risk of overgeneralizing, women clients often did better than the men. They listened and followed instructions carefully, and their egos didn't interfere. Many male clients of that era were CEOs or other management types who were accustomed to making the decisions. This could raise problems on a climb, where these men were relegated to follower status.

"Why are you going to the right? Why don't we go to the left? It looks shorter to go that way," we'd hear.

At times the questioning devolved into badgering, to which the guides had a ready reply: "Well, Mr. Smith, you are obviously more experienced in this business than we are. There's just one thing that baffles us."

"What's that?" Smith would say.

## AVOIDING THE SUDDEN STOP

"If you are so experienced and confident that your decisions are better than ours, why did you make such a poor decision to waste your money in hiring us?" That usually quieted down the flat-land generals.

Climbing Rainier was a dangerous business. That business necessitated clear and direct communication between guides and clients. A guided climb is not a democratic process. It's a combat maneuver. We didn't vote our way up the mountain. On the other hand, guiding strikes the best possible balance between firmness and encouragement. We understood that clients were under enormous mental stress and were out of their natural environments. A good guide walks a tightrope, balancing safety against an effort to provide clients with the most enjoyable big mountain climbing experience possible, and to summit if feasible. After all, they signed on for a summit climb.

On balance it merits relating again how remarkable it was to be able to muster a hodgepodge of ages, genders, and abilities and in a scant couple of days have them function well enough to climb to the top of Mount Rainier and back. My helmet is off to these resilient, adventurous souls—the clients.

## 31 THE DRUNK

*A drunk with an ice axe must be deftly handled.*

We summited early on a brilliant August day in 1966 with a strong party of clients. I was running a rope team of seven. Immediately behind me was a fellow named Bernie, and behind him was a rather snobbish and insufferable professor of botany from the University of Washington. These many years later, I don't recall the others on my rope, but they were strong.

On the climb up I had done a fair amount of chatting with Bernie if for no other reason than to filter out the incessant combination of philosophizing and complaining by the professor. Bernie related that he was a chef at Johnny's Dock restaurant in Tacoma, that he had grown up in the area, lived under the towering presence of Mount Rainier, and had thus made it his objective to climb it using our guide service. Unbeknownst to me this was only half of his goal.

We unroped with all of our clients at the crater rim and ambled across to sign in at Register Rock. The quarter-mile diameter of the snow-filled crater served as a giant pen where clients could move about freely unroped and in relative safety. Having summited before noon, we were able to take more time to eat our lunches, rest, and rehydrate.

At one o'clock in the afternoon, we herded the clients back across the crater and roped them up for the long climb down. In the first hundred feet or so, I noticed something different about both Bernie and the professor. The professor had allowed his throat to dry out; he continued his complaining, but now his voice was just an amusing croak. Bernie, normally cryptic, was now talking freely and loudly. He was also just a touch unsteady. Initially I chalked this up to common fatigue in the legs, but as we moved haltingly down the glacier and lowered our altitude, Bernie began to sway and swerve and slur his words. Could he be having an attack of cerebral edema? I quickly stopped the team, coiled my rope up next to Bernie, and looked in his eyes.

"Bernie, Are you okay?"

"I'm jushed fine," he said. The smell of hop-laden alcohol wafted with the words.

"Bernie slide up your sunglasses and look at me. Have you been drinking beer?"

"Yep," Bernie responded, quickly lowering the sunglasses back over his bloodshot eyes.

"How many beers did you have?"

"Four."

"Crap! Give me the end of your prusik sling." I clipped his sling into the carabiner on my waist. This was a way of short-roping a client in need of extra assistance. If Bernie wobbled off to the right, I could give a sharp tug to the left to get him back on course. Similarly, if Bernie tried to sit down, I could give a sharp tug up on his prusik sling to keep him on his feet.

Off we went. At least Bernie was feeling no pain. The botany professor in front of Bernie croaked his complaints.

"Shut up you old bastard!"

"Now Bernie, don't talk to your fellow rope-mate that way," I said.

Bernie tossed his head back and loudly proclaimed, "I've been listening to that old fart piss and moan the whole time, and I'm tired of it."

"OK, Bernie, I understand. We've got a long way to go today before we hit the parking lot, and we all need to be a team and get along the best we can."

"Just tell him to shut up, or I'm gonna stick my ice axe up his—"

"Take it easy, Bernie," I interrupted. "Let's move."

The professor apparently heeded Bernie's advice, because he mostly quieted down. When he did croak out, Bernie would shout, "Shut up, old man," and I would have to repeat my admonishments to Bernie. So it went on that long day's descent as we staggered and lurched our way back to Camp Muir. Bernie's head finally cleared, and when we took a quick rest break at Pebble Creek en route to Paradise and the parking lot, I sat down next to him.

"Why did you sneak the beer up the mountain?"

"Well." Bernie shrugged, leveling me with a now clear and rueful eye. "Remember when I told you that I always wanted to climb Mount Rainier? That was only half of my goal. The other half was to drink a Rainier beer on top of Rainier."

"But, Bernie, it's one thing to drink one Rainier beer up there, but why four?"

Again Bernie shrugged. "Because I carried four full cans up there, and I wasn't going to carry three full cans back."

Bernie's logic was unassailable. It was my turn to shrug. I stood up and turned away; I didn't want him to see me smile.

# 32  THE FLOWER

*A flower by any other name can get you in trouble.*

Work in the RGS in the '60s encompassed more than summit trips and mountain seminars. I also taught one-day climbing schools and glacier travel and crevasse rescue out on the Nisqually and ran trips to the Paradise Ice Caves. The trail to and through the caves was a lucrative part of RGS business because it was very popular with tourists. A normal day of a guide's ice cave duties entailed two four-mile round trips to them a day, morning and afternoon.

The trail meandered across Edith Creek Basin among streams and alpine flowers, then switchbacked up over Mazama Ridge toward the caves. The flowers along the route included brilliant red Indian paintbrush and bear grass. I did not know the Latin names of either of them.

I also had a problem remembering bear grass, because the plant didn't look like grass. It had a large "poofy" white flower on a single tall stalk. On this particular sparkling day in August 1967, I was walking twenty clients along the path, trying alternately to stay awake and to engage and entertain. People of all ages, ethnicities, and persuasions were on the hike.

"This bright red plant here on the right is Indian paintbrush." As I obligingly stopped to allow pictures, I noticed a tall silver-haired gentleman paying particular attention. He was snapping away with a macro lens on an expensive camera. A shrill whistle was heard in the still air.

"That, folks, is a furry marmot. See him sunning himself on the rock over there? When he wants to communicate with his neighbors, he stands upright and whistles."

A couple of young, good-looking French women pointed excitedly. "Oh, yes, look, see Brigitte, it is the leetle furry marrmote!" I looked, and their underarms were furry. That killed my fertile imagination.

We walked on.

"And this big white flower over on the right is..." My mind drew a complete blank. I started again. "This big white flower is called..." Another long pause, and I heard myself say "elephant's breast."

There was a choking sound from the back of the group. The silver-hared man was turning apoplectic trying to bluster out his words. "It's not an elephant's breast!" he roared incredulously. "It is—" he pronounced a long Latin name "—commonly known as bear grass. There is no such plant as elephant's breast. Who told you it was elephant's breast?" He was glaring at me over his glasses. All faces turned my way.

"Sir, I normally take people up the mountain. I'm just the substitute guide on this trip for today, and I thought I was told that this big poofy white flower was named elephant's breast."

"Well, there's no excuse for not knowing your flowers, young man. And they're not 'poofy.' There's no such term as 'poofy' in botany."

"Sir, are you a botanist?" I asked.

"Yes, young man. I am the head of the botany department at Washington State University."

"I see, sir, that I stand corrected by a true expert. Would you consent to lead us in showing us the flowers here?" The professor mumbled his approval and quickly had his audience immersed in the particulars of the alpine flora. He became quite long winded, which got us back to the Paradise Inn an hour later than scheduled, but I had avoided a flower-naming conundrum.

To my surprise, after the walk several clients came up, patted me on the back, and gave me generous tips. One elderly lady handed me the money and said with a twinkle in her eye, "Elephant's breast. That was a good one!"

## 33 THE CREVASSE

*"I found myself chust schpinning through schpace..."*
–Helmut

Our guided party had just negotiated the laddered section of the Ingraham Glacier. It was dark with a new moon. Headlamps wended torturously up, traversed briefly to the right, and then dropped down past a huge angled crevasse bordering the on-ramp to Disappointment Cleaver. I had seven clients on my rope team. When climbing up and around this crevasse I was leading. This was appropriate for moving up, but in this short section I had four hundred feet of gold line in which some of my clients were down-climbing with me over a collapsed serac that formed a snow bridge over the crevasse, while others were traversing across above us. A still small voice told me to look back. At that instant, John, the second to the last client fell off the traverse, pulling my end client, Helmut, off with him. The headlamps, which a moment before were on the trail, were now bouncing crazily toward the yawning crevasse. "Run!" I yelled back to my team. I took off downhill, attempting to take up the slack in the rope created by the fall. I ran twenty feet and the rope came tight. I sprawled into a self-arrest. Glancing back along my team I counted five, all in self-arrests. The big crevasse behind the fifth client was lit up in beautiful blue hues like a Chinese lantern. "Hey Bob," I called out to Schaeffer, guiding the next rope. His team was coiling in to traverse across the base of Disappointment Cleaver.

"What's up?"

"I've got two of my clients in a crevasse. Come over and put in a belay so we can get up." Bob unroped from his team, and walked over to assess the situation. "Yup, you've got two in the crevasse. That's pretty good, Heuston. I've never seen a two-in-one before." Bob set the belay on our rope next to the crevasse. "I can't breathe!" A muffled voice was screaming from the hole. Bob shouted down, "Take it easy Helmut. If you can scream you can breathe. You're fine. It's just uncomfortable on your waist. We'll have you out in no time."

"OK," came Helmut's resigned reply.

Number six client, the one who fell, pulling off Helmut, was surprisingly quiet. "You OK John?" I asked. I was up at the lip with Bob. We scanned the gold line between the fallen clients. It was lodged on the

## AVOIDING THE SUDDEN STOP

serac snow bridge. "George, you lucked out," Schaeffer observed. One client fell one side of the bridge, and one fell on the other side. They balanced each other out." I peered down.

Figure 4 The author crossing a snow bridge on the Tahoma Glacier similar to the one straddled by two clients on the Ingraham in 1967.

Sure enough, Helmut and John were hanging in the crevasse almost facing each other with the snow bridge above and in between. They looked like sausages strung on a hook. If our party had been comprised of only one or two three-man rope teams we might have experienced serious difficulties with the rescue. But we had thirteen strong clients at hand, with more on the Cleaver if needed. Bob slid his ice axe under the rope by the lip of the crevasse and yelled "Pull!" The five of us on the rope merely walked downhill and pulled first John, and then Helmut out of their blue big hole. We brushed ourselves off and quickly followed Schaeffer's team onto the rocks of Disappointment Cleaver. We needed to catch up with the rest of the party. At the top of the Cleaver we took our usual break as the sun rose. The climb thereafter was completed in good order, with the exception of Helmut. Helmut was an attorney. He lived in Seattle, but grew up in Germany. He thus had a heavy German accent, and endlessly that day, Helmut excitedly re-told his story to anyone venturing near: "I vas valking along, everyting vas gute, and zen I found myself chust schpinning through scpace!"

"OK, Helmut, you and John did good. You walked away from an unbelievable fall completely unhurt," I'd say, trying to get Helmut to shut up and settle down.

"Ya, it vas amazing zat I vas unhurt. And Chon too. He fell, pulled me off, and I found myzelf chust schpinning through schpace!" Helmut remained animated for the rest of the trip. He never did shut up. Why should he? After all, he'd survived "schpinning through schpace." He had avoided the sudden stop.

## 34  The Ladders

*"Seems secure to me."* –Fred Stanley

The Ingraham Glacier–Disappointment Cleaver summit route up Mount Rainier was disintegrating. Above the Ingraham Flats, snow bridges were collapsing as crevasses pulled farther apart. Snowfall the previous winter had been sparse. The entrance ramp to the bottom of Disappointment Cleaver, never a safe place, experienced increased rockfall.

"I bought two twenty-four-foot aluminum ladders. Who wants to take them up to install on the Ingraham before tomorrow's climb?" Jack Melill's question was followed by silence among the guides around him at the RGS store at Paradise. "OK, whoever volunteers to take the ladders up will get tomorrow off." John Rutter and I volunteered.

We went out to the parking lot, put on our packs, and a ladder was rigged on top of each of them. Jack looked at us. "The Camp Muir fire department is on its way," he laughed.

Rutter and I loped off up the trail toward Muir, using the first half-mile to learn how to balance and stabilize our ungainly loads. The sides of the ladders rested on our packs and shoulders. Our heads stuck up through the rungs.

"Hey, George, you almost knocked me over. Watch out where you swing that thing," Rutter complained.

"Then quit asking me questions where I have to turn around," I said. "Spread out."

Slogging up the trail to Panorama Point, both John and I rammed our ladders into rocks. The sound of the crash was transferred noisily from the point of contact along the aluminum sides past our ears. Once we gained the snowfields above Pebble Creek we could hike parallel to each other. We were an odd sight.

Hikers coming down asked, "What are those for?"

"There's a fire up on the mountain, and we have to get to it," Rutter would say.

"Where?"

"See that wisp of smoke up on the rocks there?" I'd point obscurely toward Gibraltar.

"No, I don't," the bewildered hiker would say.

"Well, it's there, and it's the park's policy to put out all fires," Rutter would say in a deep official-sounding voice as we trudged away up the hill. "Move along now."

## AVOIDING THE SUDDEN STOP

We reached Camp Muir at two o'clock that afternoon. Guide Fred Stanley, who was leading the next day's summit climb, roped up with us and we continued on to the Ingraham Glacier.

"You can dump them here," Fred said, standing next to a big crevasse with a broken snow bridge. Rutter and I dug out the extra ropes, aluminum pickets, and five-pound sledgehammers we'd also packed up. We clipped a rope and carabiner into the top rung of the first ladder. Standing it on end, we used the rope to drop the far end of the ladder down, drawbridge style. Its twenty-four-foot aluminum length only allowed for two feet to spare on each side of the crevasse. We hammered pickets into our end and secured it with rope.

"Belay me," Stanley said. Rutter gave him a boot-axe belay. John and I figured that Fred would do the sane thing: hunker down, straddle the ladder, and scoot across. Instead, Fred calmly stood on the rungs, crampons clanging, and walked over to the other side. He pulled out pickets, hammer, and rope, and secured the uphill end. "OK, let's get the next one," he said. John and I straddled the ladder and pulled ourselves across with the second one. A hundred feet farther up, we stopped and installed the second ladder. Fred stood up and walked back over both of them. On the last one, he stood in the middle and did a little jig. "Seems plenty secure to me," he said.

Duly impressed, Stanley, Rutter, and I went back down to Camp Muir.

"You two climbing with the group tomorrow?" Fred asked, grabbing a cup of coffee at the guide hut.

"Nope," Rutter said. "You've got Sprenger and Hebert with you for that. Jack gave us the day off tomorrow and we ain't spending it on the hill." With that John and I loped off down the Muir snowfield. It was late afternoon. Rutter and I jogged all the way down to Pebble Creek then ambled down the trail to Paradise. The inn dining room was just serving dinner when we walked in the entrance.

"What do you say we splurge tonight and eat in the dining room?" John suggested.

"Great idea. But let's grab a beer in the Glacier Room first."

John Rutter and I slept through our entire day off. By then rumors had circulated among the tourists that a park ranger ladder crew had scrambled to put out a fire way up on the mountain. John and I had no idea how that one got started.

## 35 THE CRATER BOWL

*"Respect. All I want is a little respect."*
–Rodney Dangerfield

Sometimes frustrations mounted between RGS guides and other parties on the mountain. Often the other parties were from organized climbing clubs, such as the Seattle Mountaineers or the Mazamas out of Portland, Oregon. During my tenure at RGS in the mid-1960s, the National Park Service rangers imposed no limits on party sizes. Thus, at various popular times during the climbing summer, Camp Muir would be swarming with RGS clients and club and private climbers. On a Fourth of July weekend, it was common for the RGS alone to be handling a summit party of forty. Similarly, the Mountaineers and Mazamas could each have fifty or more.

Tent villages sprang up, starting on the Muir snowfield and spilling over Camp Muir onto the adjacent Cowlitz Glacier. We quipped that all the rocks at Muir were replaced with people. This was not far off the mark. As clients and others stumbled around in the darkness getting ready to rope up, it was common to hear a shout or scream as people stepped on occupied sleeping bags with their crampons. That was a real wake-up call.

The Mountaineers, Mazamas, and other climbing clubs would wait for the RGS guides to leave camp for the summit, because the guides knew the route. When we roped up, they did too. Looking back we could see a Christmas string of headlamps draped out for a mile. This meant that everyone was bunched up, stepping on others' ropes, or even trying to hook in with the wrong group. It drove us nuts. We would get this sorted out and our clients on the way, but by the time we would coil up to climb to Cathedral Gap, portions of other groups would already be mixed in with ours. One could not tell if the man in front was friend or foe, and climbing courtesies dictated that parties did not intermix. There were enough hazards on the climb without adding confusion to them, but abundant confusion there would inevitably be.

"Who are you with?" The enquirer's headlamp fixed a figure in its beam.

Blinded, the figure would answer "The Mazamas," or "The Seattle Mountaineers," or "The guide service."

## AVOIDING THE SUDDEN STOP

These mix-ups could continue for hours along the summit route, until daylight mercifully allowed a sorting out.

It was with these frustrations in mind that the Crater Bowl was conceived and executed. The idea was to do a summit trip with an all-guide party—emphasis on the "party." Six or seven guides, as many as could be spared by owner Jack Melill, who empathized, would leave Camp Muir for the top. Invariably a Mountaineer or Mazama party would be looking to follow. We would let them.

Figure 5 Frank Maranville and Ben Kable inside Mount Rainier's summit crater, 1957.

We started in the usual slow, plodding manner, but as we gained the crux of the route on the Ingraham Glacier and Disappointment Cleaver, we would speed up. The Mountaineers and Mazamas would be left far behind. In 1968 we summited Rainier in four and a half hours, carrying such alpine necessities as lawn chairs, watermelons, junk food, a football, a Playboy magazine, and, of course, beer. We would sack out and rest during the time it took the other parties to summit. Then, just as each team dragged itself over the crater rim, the first view it had was of guides throwing the football around, and others sitting in lawn chairs, drinking beer, eating watermelon, and reading *Playboy*. What a sight we presented!

Looking back, it seems a bit of a harsh thing to do, to contrast and belittle the significant accomplishments of other climbers who successfully summited Mount Rainier. They greeted our scene with scowls. But we were young, strong, precocious, and wanting a bit of payback for all the other frustrating climbs we'd tolerated running chronically afoul of the Mountaineers and Mazamas, who had a knack for worming in among us. The Crater Bowl was that payback. And it was as sweet as the watermelon juice running off our chins. Just a little respect. That's all we wanted.

## 36  THE LITTLE JEWEL

*"It's better than a compass if you know your reference points." –BFH*

"What's our altitude?" guide Dave Stelling called back. We had climbed into a cloud cap covering the summit dome of Mount Rainier.

"I'm reading thirteen thousand, seven hundred and fifty feet," I replied. "We may be a little higher than what the altimeter reads due to a bit of low pressure."

"When did you reset it last?"

"At the top of Disappointment Cleaver, so there shouldn't be much more than fifty feet of error in the reading." Stelling nodded and plodded on. I set an additional wand on the trail marking the altitude as a waypoint for our return. Between the wands, which were placed every rope length in the glacier, and the altimeter, we had the route nailed for navigating our return.

Dad had bought me a Thommen pocket altimeter for work at the RGS. "The Little Jewel," as BFH fondly called it, was our primary means of navigation on the big volcanic peaks of the Northwest. The Thommen was exceedingly accurate. It measured altitude within fifty vertical feet. If a climber carried a topographical map or otherwise knew the elevations of prominent land features, the Little Jewel worked better than a compass. I kept the altimeter on a lanyard around my neck and inside my shirt pocket for ready referral. The analogue outer dial displayed prominent graduations at five-hundred-foot intervals up to three thousand feet. Between those intervals were fifty- and hundred-foot tick marks. Smaller circular inner scales read "Pressure in inches of Mercury," and outside that, pressure in millibars, thereby providing a barometric reading. A fine needle pointer depicted the rise and fall of pressure or altitude on the display. As a climber ascended, the needle would move clockwise, reflecting higher altitude, and swing counterclockwise when descending. There was also a small color-coded inner window. As we climbed above three thousand feet, the needle on the Thommen would swing full circle. Like a shifting gear, the little inner window would roll over from a red "zero" to a yellow "three," indicating that the climber had passed three thousand feet and should now read the "one thousand" mark on the outer scale as four thousand feet of altitude.

## AVOIDING THE SUDDEN STOP

A little blue "six" with a needle reading of 2,250 thus recorded the climber at 8,250 feet. These little colored gradations required attention, because if interpreted carelessly, one could be 3,000 feet off in reading the altimeter. It has happened. My Little Jewel was good to fifteen thousand feet, perfect for work on Mount Rainier.

The outer ring of the Thommen was a moveable bezel allowing for recalibration. At Camp Muir, 10,060 feet, and just prior to beginning a climb, I would rotate the bezel to 10,050 feet. I was now dialed in. At the top of Disappointment Cleaver at 12,400 feet, I would rotate the bezel again to align the Little Jewel with the map altitude. At the bergschrund and summit I would recalibrate again, depending on visibility. In this fashion, the Thommen acted as an invaluable waypoint marker. Of course, it was also a barometer heralding weather changes. If the Little Jewel was reading higher than a known point, that meant lower pressure and a falling barometer. If it read lower, then the barometer was rising.

In the old pre-GPS days of the '60s, my Swiss Thommen altimeter kept our parties oriented and on course. And it didn't even have a battery. It was indeed the Little Jewel.

# 37 THE ICE CAVES RECOVERY

*When a cave becomes a cathedral.*

The ice caves were located two miles east of Paradise Inn at the snout of the Paradise Glacier. They were formed by wind blowing down off of surrounding cliffs at just the right angle to follow a major stream under the glacier. These following winds eventually hollowed out a labyrinth of ice caves over a mile in length. The entrance to the caves was fifteen feet high. As clients were walked back into them, the outside sun shone through the ice, turning the light a translucent blue. A hundred feet or more in, the caves became pitch-black. We carried a Coleman lantern in our packs to show clients how the light shimmered off the myriad angled surfaces. Small streams flowed through each cave, adding airy burbling white noise to the stillness.

One afternoon in early August of 1967, guide John Rutter came running into the guide service office. "One of our clients collapsed in the caves and Jay Sprenger sent me to get help."

Owner Jack Melill grabbed a portable oxygen canister and shoved it in my hand. "George, get up to the caves with this. Jack, you go with him and take an extra medical kit. I'll grab a couple of other guides and follow right behind with a radio and the akja."

An akja was a light packable aluminum stretcher shaped like a shallow boat with two long handles extending from each end. On snow the akja was a sled. On hard ground it came with a pneumatic wheel a little smaller than a bicycle tire that was attached underneath so bearers could roll it while balancing the akja with the handles. The wheel then bore the balance of the patient's weight.

Jack Hebert and I jogged up the Edith Creek Basin trail and over Mazama Ridge to the cave entrance. Switching on our headlamps, we stepped back into the darkness and shouted, "Jay, where are you?"

Jay's muffled voice came back to us. We followed it to where the cave split, and took the left-hand fork. We found Sprenger and his party five hundred feet back. The roof of the cave was beginning to taper down to head height. We could now see the light of a Coleman lantern, and when we rounded the corner we saw Jay straddling a client on the ground. The rest of the dozen or so clients huddled around Jay. The man on the

## AVOIDING THE SUDDEN STOP

ground was tall, perhaps in his late fifties. We got the oxygen out, put it on the man, and adjusted the mask. A red foam was oozing from the man's mouth as Jay continued his CPR. I took Jay's place.

"What happened?" I asked.

"I was doing the tour here, and I heard moaning. I looked back, and my client just fell over." Jay looked down at me through tired, bloodshot eyes. "The man's wife is here with us."

"What's her name?"

"Mabel."

"And his?"

"Melvin."

I asked Jack Hebert to move the rest of the clients back a few more feet to clear the way for the team coming with the akja and radio. Melvin's eyes were fixed and dilated. His skin was ice-cold and his limbs were going rigid.

Melvin was dead. Whatever caused his death was massive and quick. He likely died just a few minutes after collapsing. The problem at the moment was how to handle his wife. She was sobbing quietly at Melvin's side. I looked back at Jay and could now detect outlines of grief etched in his face along with the fatigue. Jay had also known the situation was fatal only minutes after the event, but he couldn't bring himself to tell Melvin's wife. She, like Melvin, was tall and also middle-aged. Her prim brunette hair was now falling in disheveled strands around her tear-stained face. She loved Melvin.

The couple had started their day in Paradise. They had taken a happy sunlit walk to the ice caves with our guide service. Her happy walk with her husband was over now, forever.

"Mabel," I said. "While I work on Melvin, would you please massage his legs?"

"OK," she said. "Oh, his legs are so cold." She sobbed quietly.

"Excuse me." A short wiry man stepped forward from the huddle of clients. "My name is Father Mark. I am a Catholic priest. I do not want to interfere, but if you wish, I can administer the last rites for Melvin."

"Right here?" Mabel asked quietly.

"Yes, Mabel, right here."

"Does that mean my husband is dead?"

"No," said Father Mark. "It is meant to pray for him, and for you, and to give you both peace." Mabel slowly nodded her assent. And right there in the caves, as we went through the motions of first aid in their depths, and by the hissing light of a Coleman lantern, Father Mark dipped his hands in the little stream, put his hands on Melvin's head, and solemnly performed the last rites of the Roman Catholic Church.

The minute Father Mark finished, the backup rescue crew arrived with the akja. We loaded Melvin on it, and with me riding the sled and continuing CPR, we dragged him out of the caves into the bright light of day. Jack Melill radioed for a helicopter from McChord Air Force Base. It was already en route. Fifteen minutes later the heavy whopping sounds of rotor blades echoed the inbound HH-43 Huskie's arrival. It was a high-altitude machine with twin canted counter rotating blades. The ship landed. A paramedic ran over and waved the akja over. We loaded client Melvin, with his good and grieving wife, Mabel. The HH-43 lifted off, nosed around a corner, and was gone.

Figure 6 Paradise Ice Caves, 1967.

The walk back to camp was quiet, as people seemed to be in a pensive mood. John Rutter had taken the other clients back to Paradise before the HH-43 arrived—all except Father Mark, who ambled along quietly by my side. He had remained with Mabel to help escort her into the helicopter. I reflected on this man. Who could have predicted that the one time we suffered a fatality on a trip to the ice caves a priest would be there? It all seemed preordained. Maybe a shoulder angel materialized that day to perform a special mission of comfort.

I often reflect on the sad scene of that summer day in the caves—the day caverns became cathedrals and softly eased a loving couple through doorways of life and death.

## 38 THE "GIB" ROUTE

*Gibraltar is a mountain of rock in the Mediterranean. A mountain of rocks on Rainier is The Gib.*

The standard route up the Ingraham Glacier and Disappointment Cleaver fell apart in the summer of '67. Crevasses got too wide, and the snow bridges over them collapsed. We patched the trail with twenty-four-foot aluminum ladders, but eventually even they would not fit across the biggest holes. The park service shut down the mountain for all private climbs, and the guide service was the only outfit permitted to run summit trips; but that was with the proviso that we had to use the Gibraltar route to bypass the broken standard routes.

The Gibraltar, or "Gib" route (pronounced "Jib"), transports climbers to the 12,300-foot level on Rainier.

It was used extensively in the earlier alpenstock-hobnailed boot days of mountaineering and on up into the 1930s, when a section of ledge on the primary route calved away. Viewed from Paradise, Gibraltar Rock is a prominent outcrop that dominates the Rainier's southeastern skyline. It is not a solid rock like a Yosemite's granite Half Dome, but is rather a shambles of crumbling basalt cliffs and ledges. Great icicles festoon Gibraltar's upper rim, resulting from the freeze-thaw cycle that begets relentless rock and icefalls. Many of these events are jaw-dropping in scale. It is common to witness avalanches or landslides off of Gib's flanks that span hundreds of yards, composed of ice blocks and rocks the size of cars.

The keys to the Gib route are its ledges. Rubble-strewn and airy, they are relatively safe if teams properly coil in their ropes and bunch up, climbing close in against the overhanging cliffs above. For decades a handy ledge leading just above Camp Misery atop the Cowlitz Glacier at eleven thousand feet was the standard guided route. It curled along the middle of Gibraltar and exited into a steep ice chute that formed the eastern boundary of the Nisqually Glacier. This is known, predictably, as the Gibraltar Chute. A portion of the "standard" ledge collapsed in 1938. This left a gap that became a rappel point to the next ledge thirty feet below. Rappels are a fine expedient under normal climbing conditions with an unguided party; they are anathema to a guided group, because clients lack requisite skill and confidence to do a rappel in the dark, during the ascending early hours. This Gib rappel point was also directly exposed to rockfall.

For a few weeks in 1967, we installed a ladder at the rappel site, but it was a long one, and clients struggling in the dark would take interminable amounts of time negotiating it. Herding a guided party of twenty or thirty clients through this choke point could add as much as four hours to a summit climb.

All that imagination could conjure occurred there. I've seen clients slip off a rung, fall, and lodge upside down with body, ropes, and ladder all cat-cradled together. This inevitably led to a cacophony of screaming clients and yelling guides. Swearing colored the darkness along with the feeble bobbing rays of headlights playing in all directions along the cliffs. Add to this the periodic "Rock!" warnings accompanying the normal roughage falling from Gibraltar's upper heights, and the perfect emotional storm began to spread its magic. Much of a guide's job at this point consisted of reassuring chatter coupled with the occasional firm command: "Jim, you're doing great. Hold on to your rope coils now, and stay closed up with Bill." "Dave, you dodged that rock like a cat. I'm proud of you!" "John, this isn't the place to sit down. Get up!" On it went, hour after hour as the party wove its ponderous way along the ledges. Finally, as the eastern sky began to lighten, we would arrive at the chute.

The Gibraltar Chute was yet another funnel for falling rock and ice. Three steep, long rope-lengths comprised its crux. Bordered on its western edge by the Nisqually Glacier's icefall, cliffs of hanging ice, and on the east by Gibraltar Rock, the Chute was a snow gully that stabbed upward at a forty-five-degree angle. Often the Chute's condition varied from deep sun-cupped snow, which snagged ropes and tripped climbers, to bands of hard ice, where crampon points barely dented its surface. Also, the Chute didn't just terminate at the route's high access point off the Gib ledges, but continued straight down another 1,500 feet. When clients were in the Chute they thus were continually exposed, not only to crumbling rock and ice fall from upper Gibraltar, but also to the threat of a long fall down the Chute and a sudden stop at the end.

Guide Don McPherson and I tried fixing ropes. We strung line, built snow bollard anchors, and set ice screws, to no great purpose, other than psychological. The setup would not survive more than one hot day. We could take a party up the Chute on secure fixed line in the morning, and by the time we returned in the afternoon the ice screws would be melted out, laying sideways on the snow.

One day guide Jay Ullin and I descended from the summit to the Chute with a party of fourteen clients. That meant we were two teams of eight. We didn't want to subject an entire rope team to the exposure of the Chute, so we roped the party together into one group about six hundred feet long. That allowed us to have at least one guide and some clients anchoring everyone up on the flatter, more secure ground of the Upper Nisqually Glacier while the leading elements of the party were down-climbing the Chute. Conversely, as the leading climbers reentered the Gibraltar ledges, they kept walking, thus providing a "moving belay" for those bringing up the rear. It was slow, but effective. Several falls were easily arrested.

The Gib route was especially exhausting for both clients and guides. It once took one of my groups thirteen hours to summit Rainier. A normal climb to the top was eight hours. Another guided climb dragged itself back to the Muir huts a whopping twenty-two hours after leaving them. The Gib route thus earned its reputation among the guides as "The Marathon." Looking back on the 1967 Gib route many years hence, it is a wonder we never lost or injured anyone. Only by the good graces of shoulder angels were we able to avoid the falling rocks and sudden stops.

Late one moonlit night that summer, several of us were standing out by the Paradise Inn and happened to glance up at the mountain. Out of the blackness that defined Gibraltar, we spotted a light blinking out an SOS. It was being repeated. Bad news. We awoke the climbing rangers, and RGS manager Jack Melill. "Let's try to raise the guides at Muir," he said.

For an hour we called Camp Muir, but their radio was off. This was normal back in those days before cell phones. Radio contact was only established with Camp Muir once a week on a fixed schedule. This was because the old "portable" Motorola Park Service radio stowed up there was the size of a bread box, weighed thirty pounds, and devoured batteries.

"It looks like we've got to go up there," Jack said. The rangers agreed, and up the hill we went. Our mixed guide-ranger rescue patrol reached Muir at about one o'clock in the morning and, together with two guides already at Muir, we roped up and headed up the Cowlitz Glacier toward Gib and Camp Misery. A couple of hours later, we spotted bobbing headlamps moving down toward us. Two young male climbers met us near the top of the Cowlitz.

"Were you guys sending out an SOS?" Jack Melill asked.

"Yes," one of them casually responded.

"Why?"

"Well, we summited via Disappointment Cleaver but decided the crevasses were too dangerous on that route, so we decided to come back down through Gibraltar."

A ranger's voice, beginning to rise in anger, said, "Jack, I'll handle this. Why were you broadcasting an SOS?"

"Because we got onto the ledges and thought we might be lost. But then we sat down, had a bite to eat and a drink of water, and while we were sitting there we spotted a wand. So we found the route and now we're fine," they said.

## AVOIDING THE SUDDEN STOP

"Well, speaking of fine," the ranger replied, reaching into his back pocket and pulling out a ticket book. "I'm writing you a citation."

"What for?"

"I don't know yet. Calling for help when you really didn't need it. But mainly for being stupid and making all of us come up here. So the fine that goes with this little caper of yours will cost you three hundred dollars. How's that for 'fine'?"

The Gib route—a fine climb indeed.

# 39  Mortality's Minute

*Sewing Machine Leg, aka, The Death Wobbles, Stitching, and Elvis Syndrome.*

I had just come down from the Gibraltar Chute. It was summer, 1967. Don McPherson and I had climbed up there early that morning to put in fixed ropes. It was now midafternoon.

"George, you go back down and meet the next batch of clients coming up to Muir for tomorrow's climb. Help Sprenger get them organized."

"How long are you going to stay up here, Don?"

"Not more than another hour. I need to get a couple more ice screws in to anchor this fixed line."

I started off across the Gib ledges, climbed up the ladder we had newly positioned to avoid rockfall, and walked over to Camp Misery. Camp Misery, at 11,033 feet, sits high at the southern base of Gibraltar Rock, where it joins the Cowlitz Cleaver. I had never climbed solo before. I took a quick break, had a bite to eat, and enjoyed the sun and solitude. I had two choices for descending: the Cowlitz Glacier, which McPherson and I had climbed in the morning—the guided route; or I could climb down the Cowlitz Cleaver itself.

I had been up the Cowlitz Cleaver to Camp Misery once before with BFH. I knew that one portion of it, called the Beehive, was exposed and should require being roped up. On the other hand, descending the Cowlitz Glacier solo and unroped, over snow bridges softened by the afternoon sun, was chancy. If one broke and I fell into a crevasse, I would be a goner. I chose to climb down the rocks of the cleaver.

The Beehive is a spike in the Cowlitz Cleaver. It lay about a third of the way down my route to Camp Muir. There was one move on it that demanded calm concentration. As I scrambled the rocks leading to it, I rehearsed it in my mind. I would traverse under the Beehive on a western ledge overhanging the Nisqually Glacier and Gibraltar Chute. At the point where the ledge petered out, was "The Move"—a long reach and step up to the next ledge with the right leg, facing into the rock. There were good feet- and handholds, so there was no problem maintaining the three-point climbing stance, where feet and hands are anchored and one foot or hand is moved at a time. The problem for me was that the Move was a comfortable reach for someone six feet tall, but not for me at five-foot-ten.

I knew to be aware of my Kelty frame pack and to avoid hitting it on the overhang. That would be melancholy. Frank Maranville had lost a climbing friend that way a year before. They were on a climb in the Olympics and had not yet reached their rope-up point. The friend, a dentist whose name I can't recall, was walking under overhanging rock. He ducked his head around it fine, but the aluminum post of his frame pack, which stuck up slightly above his head, hit the rock and unbalanced him. Surprised and pushed outward, he fell off the trail to his death.

"All right, George, here you are," I said to myself. I was on the Beehive, at the Move. "Make this move with authority, and you've got it made. Use the momentum of placing your extended right leg, get secure handholds, and push off with your left toe. That will give you just enough forward movement to step up onto that right leg."

I took a deep breath and swung my right leg up, I felt the toe of my boot reach the good hold, but I hesitated. In that hesitation I was stuck, spread-eagled. I had committed my balance to my right side. I could not retrieve my right foot. The left leg and calf were straining. I looked down; it was a hundred-foot drop to the next ledge, followed by several more to the ice and crevasses of the Nisqually Glacier.

Suddenly my left leg began to bounce up and down. I was in trouble. Fatigue and fear had brought on what climbers term "sewing-machine leg," where the leg involuntarily trembles. It started out mild but swiftly intensified. If it became severe enough it would cause me to peel off my hand- and footholds and fall. Fear welled up and caught me raw in the throat. If I fall, they won't even look for me over here, I thought. They'll look on the standard route on the Cowlitz Glacier. They'll check the crevasses, but they won't find me. Our bush pilot, Jimmy Beech, will be called in to search. He'll circle, expertly playing the fickle winds of the mountain to work in close. If the weather holds, on a pass, he may catch a glimpse of my body crumpled on the rocks or glacier far below. Perhaps a glint off the metal of my ice axe. He'll circle—like a buzzard—he will circle.

"Stop it!" I heard myself shout. "Get hold of yourself! Now, transfer a little weight back to your left leg. Drop your heel down slightly below your toes and will yourself to relax." I did. Slowly, the sewing machine quieted. The violent up-and-down shaking retreated to a shiver. But now I could feel the calf of my left leg beginning to cramp up. Damn! If that happens I'm done.

"Make your move now, George," I said. My voice was calm, devoid of fear. Maybe it was my shoulder angel speaking. "You transferred a little weight back to your left leg and slowed down the shaking. So you know you have a little room to shift. Shift back to your right leg, and when you do, just continue. Step right up on your right leg, and use your right hand to pull yourself. It's in a good hold." I prayed, rocked back on my left leg, and in one step-and-pull, was up on my right leg. For a moment I stood on it, sweating and exhaling loudly. Then I switched feet. The next step with the right leg was short and easy. I was past the Beehive and back on Cowlitz Cleaver.

I don't know how long I lingered on the Move. Likely only a minute. In that minute I again came face-to-face with mortality. Shaking now, I found a flat boulder and rested; I took a long swig of water and a salt pill. If my legs were cramping up, I needed immediate rehydration. I also needed to replace the salt I'd just sweated out in such profusion. I thanked my shoulder angel and scrambled down the cleaver to Camp Muir.

"Where have you and Don been?" Jay Sprenger was angry. "It's getting late and we have to get clients organized."

"We had to move the ladder on the Gib ledge and fix ropes up in the chute," I replied wearily. Jay nodded; the anger left his face. He knew the route was a dangerous shambles and any efforts to mitigate problems were well spent.

Don McPherson arrived back at Camp Muir an hour later. "I think things are better on the route, at least for tomorrow's climb," he said.

I never mentioned my predicament up on the Beehive to anyone. There was no point in it. All who seriously climb will one day experience sewing-machine leg, Elvis syndrome, stitches, or the death wobble. It will inevitably occur on their "Move"—that one uncomfortable, fearful reach or step that defines winning or losing in the sport—life or death. It is mortality's minute.

# 40  The Green Ranger

*The green movement on Mount Rainier began here.*

"Can I stay in here with you tonight?" The face of the climbing ranger looked through the half-open Dutch door of the guide hut at Camp Muir.

"Sure, John, no sweat," I said groggily. "If you don't mind doing the cooking."

"Deal," he said.

I was sprawled on a bunk, so tired that my crampons were still on from the day's summit climb. It was my second in three days, and I was scheduled to take another party up two days later. I'm no good at math, but that figured to be three summit climbs in six days. Several days earlier I had gotten into an argument with the scheduler. Never argue with a guide service scheduler.

I awoke briefly to the comforting sound of water boiling in a pot on the propane stove and the sweet aroma of cooking macaroni. John was happily keeping his part of the bargain. Normally he camped in the William Butler A-frame shelter up in back of the guide hut, but it was cramped, and the amenities were much better in here.

It was a fine July day, but the weather was changing. After the day's climb, while I was hustling the other guides and clients off down to Paradise, I noticed that Nevermore, our resident camp raven, had spread his big wings and flown off toward lower elevations. Nevermore was a perfect barometer. If he left Camp Muir, there was sure to be a storm moving within the next few hours. And it did.

After John and I ate dinner, I crawled into a sleeping bag and was out like a light. At about eleven o'clock that night, I awoke to wind slamming the hut. "Nevermore was right again," I wearily reflected and went back to sleep.

The light of the next morning was blotted by a howling storm. Ranger John cooked up oatmeal and coffee. As we sat spooning the last of the mush off our plates, he said, "I need to go out and change the chemical toilets." At that environmentally unfriendly time in the '60s, that simply meant pulling the large canisters out of the latrines, hauling them out to a crevasse on the Cowlitz, and dumping in the contents. John paused and then asked, "Would you help me?"

"John, are you crazy? This wind is going to make that little chore impossible. Why don't you just wait a few hours until it dies down?"

John shook his head. "My boss told me it had to be done by today."

"Well," I said, "your boss isn't here, is he? He's all snug in his office down at Longmire."

"You don't know my boss," John replied grimly.

"Yes, I do. I see your dilemma, John, but it still isn't worth risking in this wind. You know we get sudden updrafts up off the Cowlitz in weather like this."

"Nope. I'm going anyway." John's mind was made up.

"OK, but I'm not going with you. Have fun," I said.

Ranger John prepared himself well for the elements. He slipped the hood up over his red down jacket and stepped out into the storm. Muir was now being hit with snow and winds gusting up to eighty miles per hour. I sat cozily in the guide hut drinking coffee and watching the fine rock dust being driven in through the old mortared rock walls of the cabin. A half hour went by. Forty-five minutes. I was just beginning to get concerned enough to put my gear on and go look for John when there was a knock at the door. I opened it. Standing there was a specter of Ranger John. He had left the guide hut with an expensive red down expedition parka. He came back with a green one. A powerful minty chemical smell came wafting in.

"You were right," John muttered resignedly.

"You look like you've been in a shit storm," I quipped. John's face did not reflect the humor of my words or his predicament. "Well, John, you're not coming in here like that. Strip down. I'll get some soap and water."

As John slowly complied, I grabbed an extra shirt and pants from his pack and took them to the lea of the hut, where he was shivering in his long johns. He put on the clean clothes and I let him in. Now he smelled only faintly of mint.

"You're OK now, John," I said. "We could use a little air freshener in here." He nodded, this time with a grateful smile. I loaned him my down parka to get him warmed back up and gave him a mug of coffee. He sipped quietly for a minute, warming his fingers on the tin cup. "So, John," I asked, breaking the awkward silence, "how did it go emptying the latrines?"

Park rangers are green. But I only met one who was that green.

# 41   THE WHITEOUT

*"A condition of diffuse light when no shadows are cast, due to a continuous white cloud layer appearing to merge with the white snow surface. No surface irregularities of the snow are visible, but a dark object may be clearly seen. There is no visible horizon." –Sir Edmond Hillary (The Crossing of Antarctica, Fuchs and Hillary, 1958)*

Our RGS party had summited; but to do so we had to climb into a large lenticular cloud capping the mountain. Lenticular clouds are formed over the high mass of the mountain, and herald, at best, unstable weather, and at worst bad. We hurriedly signed the register and started back. The cap on the top was descending with us and thickening into blowing snow. A storm had formed around Mount Rainier. What had been a clear ascent turned rapidly into a murky dull white that merged perfectly with the color of the glacier. Wind had blown old and new snow across our trail, obliterating it except for occasional bamboo marker wands with flapping red surveyor's tape. Jay Ullin put me in the lead on the way down, to find the path, with a strong client anchoring my rope team.

 I knew the route as well as any of the guides; and yet, as I cautiously edged down steepening slopes, I quickly realized that most of what I knew, or could reference, was gone—whipped away in the snow and wind. Merger of slope and sky was so complete that all of us in the party were becoming spatially disoriented. With vertigo one's head deceives—the sense of down or sideways feels like up, yet when relied upon a fall ensues. All of us did a lot of falling on this descent. My altimeter read 13,300 ft, and I knew I must be reaching the bergschrund. But this was not enough. In order to cross it I had to find the right snow bridge. It angled northeast, crossed into a series of traverses and zigzags around crevasses, then bore left (north) again before plunging east down the fall line of the Ingraham Glacier to the top of Disappointment Cleaver.

 My route-finding became a crawl. Descending from the top of a cone, such as Mount Rainier, the slightest error in direction at the beginning may amplify into many hundreds of feet of error on a descent. In no time a climber can find himself in completely unfamiliar terrain. Additionally, a relentless wind, like we experienced on this day from the southwest, can inexorably nudge climbers off course.

I was aware of all of these factors as I eased downwards, looking for anything familiar. I heard a faint buzz off to my right—the flapping of surveyors tape on a marker wand, and moved toward it. Actually it was an "X" of two crossed wands signifying the entry point to our snow bridge over the bergschrund. We were on the route. I crossed the bridge with a sense of relief. But this was brief. Beyond the bergschrund, after a left-hand traverse of two rope lengths, I began to probe for the turn back to the right around a big crevasse. The whiteout intensified. The coyote fur rim on my down parka's hood danced crazily across my face in the gusts of wind. Was that a wand I just glimpsed out of the corner of my eye? No, just the fur playing games. It was my only reference point in all-consuming white. For a moment I humored myself with the thought that the coyote that sacrificed himself for my warmth was getting even.

"George, Jay wants to know what the holdup is?" Steve, the next client behind me on my rope relayed the message down.

"Tell him I'm making the turn into the crevasse field and am trying to locate the wands," I shouted back. I knew I had to move. Clients standing in rope teams hundreds of feet behind me were getting cold. I turned east and groped my way a few feet down a steep slope. It didn't feel right, so I climbed back up and worked back to the left, probing with the shaft of my axe for hidden crevasses. For a fleeting instant my eye caught the color of red. It was just the tiniest dot off at about ten o'clock on my left. I knew it must be our wand. RGS wands were capped with red tape. I made haste for it. Sure enough it was the marker signifying the turn into the crevasse field. Things should go better now, I assured myself, once in the field, wands were placed at every rope length, and the glacier, now blanketed thickly under foot, felt like the route was here. "Don't rely on feelings," I spoke audibly to myself through my muffled parka hood, "they sometimes save, but often kill." Many an epic tale of being lost in the mountains began with a feeling of being on the right route. And yet, as I probed and plodded cautiously along, looking at the totality of white that engulfed me, I knew that my feelings were among my last-route-finding-tools left—those, and my shoulder angel.

I reached the end of my rope length, but still no wand was seen. I began to move laterally, first to the right, then back to the left, knowing that a wand must be in the vicinity. This time I came upon part of the marker's green bamboo shaft. It barely protruded from the snow, and the red tape had been ripped off of it by the wind.

"OK, good," I said, "I can make the turn back to the left." The fact that I was now among a warren of crevasses and couldn't see a trace of them touched me with foreboding. I thought I knew this route so well; but today I didn't know it at all—only that deep covered crevasses were all around me and I couldn't see them—I was in a mine field. The analogy had just crossed my mind when I took a step and plunged down up to my hips. I hollered back to my rope team to get into a self-arrest, then leaned forward, flattened my chest out on the snow, and slowly pulled myself out with the pick of my ice axe. Standing up, I glanced down into the hole made by my hips. The crevasse was blue, bottomless. Strangely, I felt some succor in it. At least it was something that could now be seen, and I hungered to see anything except variations of white. I swung a few feet to the right and found another fragment of a wand.

"Don't follow my tracks," I yelled back to Steve. "Stay to the right of them until you get to the wand, then turn left."

"OK," came his wind-dampened reply.

Another traverse back to the left should put us seven hundred feet directly above Disappointment Cleaver. The top of it was small and I didn't want to miss it. If I erred left I would take the party out onto the Emmons Glacier—to the right, down the broken ice walls of the Ingraham. I checked the Little Jewel: it read 12,900 feet. Compensating for the low pressure weather system we were in I reckoned to be at around 12,850 feet, which was the breakout point for the steep but straight downward plunge to the Cleaver. The rattling of surveyors tape in the wind confirmed that I was near the wand that marked the turn and verified that I was on-route.

Ullin and I gathered the clients around us at the top of the Cleaver.

"Great work, everyone!" Jay shouted. "We're not going to rest here, but press on down, OK?" It had taken me over two hours to reach the Cleaver in the whiteout. We were an hour behind schedule, and were likely to get further behind with the conditions. The clients nodded through their hoods and I again led off. Parts of the Cleaver's rock-spine emerged momentarily, and these reference points helped greatly to alleviate the vertigo. But now, instead of becoming unsteady from that, clients began to fall frequently due to new snow balling up in their crampons. No one slid far, but it added to our time. For once Disappointment Cleaver did not disappoint. We got down and off of it, and back out onto the Ingraham Glacier in good order. But once on the Glacier the whiteout and the storm persisted. Luckily, the wands there were better protected than higher up on the Mountain, and could be readily seen. As we made our way back across the Cowlitz Glacier from Cathedral Gap to Camp Muir, I twice found myself on my side instead of standing up. The vertigo was still at work.

By the time the RGS party had packed up and headed down the Muir snowfield to Paradise in the mid afternoon, the sun was breaking through and the fog and murk was clearing. The storm, and its accompanying whiteout, dissipated as we trudged along. Near Anvil Rock, I caught sight of our big raven, Nevermore, flying back to his summer residence at Camp Muir. The barometer was rising, and better weather was on the wing.

## 42  THE WIRE

*"That phone wire has saved my rear end several times."* –BFH

Our guided party on this climb in the waning season of 1967 included Dwight Crandell, a USGS geologist. He was conducting a volcanic risk assessment of Mount Rainier for the Park Service. That year the winter snowfall had been sparse. By the end of summer, rocks around the crater's rim were exposed more than they had been in recent memory. Crandell was interested in analyzing them for his study.

The Gib ledges kept their promise of a long climb. We summited at twelve thirty in the afternoon, and Crandell collected samples of rim rocks until two thirty.

The guided party had left Camp Muir for the summit at midnight and returned to Muir at six in the evening the next day as a building storm killed the light. Eighteen hours: the Gib route had scored another "marathon."

After packing up their gear for the hike out, the clients were hustled out of their tents.

"Keep your headlights where you can get to them," McPherson said. "You will need them again before we get back to Paradise. George, bring up the rear of the party. We've got seventeen, and I want seventeen with us at the parking lot."

Don led off. I bunched the clients up into a tight group. "The wind is getting stronger, folks. Stay right on the heels of the person in front of you. If anyone stops for any reason, holler, and we will all stop. OK?"

Remnants of daylight were rapidly sucked up into swirling snow and fog. Visibility shrank as Don navigated to Anvil Rock, then to Moon Rocks. A few hundred feet farther down he stopped and I did a head count. "Seventeen," I reported.

"Good, George, we're all together. But I can't recognize any landmarks. The snowfields we climbed up yesterday in the hot weather have melted back. More rocks have come out."

"I saw the last wand back there at Moon Rocks," I said.

"Me too. But I don't see any around here, and I don't see any tracks." It was now dark. We switched on our headlamps. Their beams were swallowed in the fog.

"Don, if we bear carefully left we should come across

the old phone line."

"What phone line?"

"There was a line between the old fire lookout at Anvil Rock and Paradise. It's still there. All we have to do is find the wire and follow it down."

McPherson bore left. We all scanned the rocks and open ground for the wire. Ten minutes later a client cried, "I found it!" Keeping sight of the phone line on our left hand, the party groped its way along down to McClure Rock and Panorama Point. We took a rest at Pan when we found the main trail to Paradise.

"George, do we have everyone with us?"

"Yes," I said. McPherson led off. I decided to double check and count the clients again. Only sixteen. I hollered to Don to stop, and I walked back along the dark, snowy trail. Fifty feet around the corner I spotted the seventeenth client shuffling along with a limp.

"Hey, Joe, why aren't you staying with us? You're supposed to keep in front of me."

"I know," Joe said flatly, "but I'm not far behind." I shined my headlamp in his eyes. He was warm enough but physically spent and lethargic.

"Take this." I pulled the medical kit out of my pack and gave him a four-hour Dexedrine pill. I looked at my watch. It was nine thirty. Joe had to be down at the parking lot by one o'clock in the morning, or he would hit the wall, be completely drained of any reserve energy, and have to be carried out. I grabbed Joe's arm and moved him back to our group.

"Seventeen is now here." I told Don of the situation with Joe and that I'd given him a Dexedrine. Don nodded and headed down. Within minutes Joe had perked up and was walking and talking with the other clients. He would be OK.

Our party finally walked into the Paradise parking lot at ten thirty. We were wet and tired. Geologist Dwight Crandell safely brought back his rock samples. Seventeen clients went up the mountain, and seventeen walked back. It was a close call. I almost lost a client, and it was a lesson—never assume everyone is accounted for. Count the heads. Then count them again. McPherson also learned a secret for descending safely from Camp Muir on a dark and stormy night: Follow the wire.

## 43 Rapping the Inn

*An inn is a place of comfort. Unless you choose the wrong place to drop in.*

Guides in the 1960s at the RGS were required to participate in the park seasonal employees' talent show put on at the inn every night. RGS owners Jack Melill (1966–67) and John Anderson (1968) believed that their stand-up presentation of twenty minutes or so was good advertising.

Midway through the show, which was composed of Rainier Park summer employees doing skits, singing, or playing instruments, the guides' moment arrived. Perched high in the open log loft of the inn, and out of sight of most of the audience, we would rappel out of the rafters onto the stage floor. I used the old dulfersitz rappel, which entailed neither slings, harnesses, nor carabiners. The doubled gold line rope was simply passed between the front legs, looped back over a hip across the chest to the opposite shoulder, and crossed again down the back where the hip hand controlled the rate of descent. The other hand was held chest high and controlled the uphill or anchor side of the rope. The dulfersitz rappel method thus used the surface area of the legs and torso for braking friction. It was simple and elegant. Sometimes we would rappel out of the rafters, stop in midair fifteen feet above the floor, and give our presentations. When we had completed our pitch for RGS services, we would finish the rappel, step out of the rope, and leave the stage to make way for the next act.

On the stage sat a big beautiful custom-built piano sporting a frame of elaborately carved and highly polished natural wood with vertical posts on its four corners—posts, as I was to rediscover, that were sharpened to spearlike points at the top.

One night as I made my entrance, stepped off into the rappel, and was swinging freely in midair, I discovered to my chagrin that I was hanging directly over one of the piano's wicked sharp posts. I looked around at the employees mixed in with the guests. They were splitting with laughter. I had been pranked and was now in an uncomfortable predicament.

"Hi, folks. Welcome to Mount Rainier, this beautiful rustic inn, and this damned nasty piano." The guests roared with laughter. "You know, I had a whole shtick

## AVOIDING THE SUDDEN STOP

for you tonight, but when I look down I find it a bit difficult to concentrate. In fact," I said glancing down, "there's only one thing on my mind and it's rather sharp." More gales of laughter. "Folks, the first rule of mountaineering is planning. The first rule of rappelling is to know what's at the bottom. Since I have obviously broken both of those rather fundamental rules tonight, I must say to you that in all honesty, and as a guide for the Rainier Guide Service, you should definitely think twice about using our services." Howls of laughter ensued. I was beginning to sweat, and the employees loved every minute of it.

Figure 7
The pointy piano.

"Is there a piano mover in the house? How about that big strong young man over there in the corner? Can you move the piano for me?" He shook his head. More peals of laughter. Finally, after what seemed an eternity, a couple of employees scurried out on stage and rolled the monster out from under my landing zone. I completed the rappel, stepped out of the rope, bowed, and walked off the stage.

Always know what's at the bottom of a rappel. It prevents sudden—or painful—stops.

## 44 THE LOVE

*Beware the moonlit night, if to Paradise you are heading. For the end of a siren evening may lead to a shotgun wedding.*

"What's the matter, Herb?" Gary Ullin asked. Guide Herb Staley's eyes were wild, glancing. Gary, Jay Ullin, and I clustered around him.

"She's after me."

"Who?"

"That waitress from the dining room."

It was ten o'clock on Saturday night at the crowded Paradise Inn. "I Want to Hold Your Hand," by the Beatles, blared from the jukebox. The dance floor was full. Love was in the air.

"What waitress?" Ullin pried. "Can you point her out?"

"No!" Staley said under his breath. "That'll just make it worse."

"OK, then, just tip your head in her direction."

"Two o'clock," Herb muttered with a tiny nod to his right.

"That's Corinne," Jay said, catching sight of the petite brunette over by the gift shop doors. "She's beautiful. Why would you run from her?" Jay's question expressed sincere puzzlement.

"We danced once last night. She was all over me," Herb said, eyes darting.

"What's wrong with that?" Gary asked.

"Ever since, she won't let me out of her sight," Herb said, ignoring Gary's question. "If I go in the men's restroom, she's there when I come out. If I dance with another girl, she's right there crowding, staring at me." We took discreet turns looking at Corinne. She was stealing looks at Herb.

"She's stalking me. See her over at the doors of the gift shop? She watches for me in the reflection of the glass. If I move, she moves. If I go outside, she goes outside. It's creepy. You guys have to get me out of here," Herb pleaded.

The Ullin brothers put their heads together. "OK," Gary said. "Here's what we'll do. I'll go choose a slow dance. Herb, you sit down in the chair right here. Look relaxed. Jay and George will stand next to you. When I dance with Corrine, she'll see you in the chair and assume you're not going anywhere. I'll chat her up, distract her, and keep her back to you. When I nod, Herb, you stand up, take off your guide sweater, and walk out the back way. Jay and George, you go with Herb and screen him."

The plan worked perfectly. Gary pulled Corinne close to him. The song was "Smoke Gets in Your Eyes." Gary nodded over. Herb sprang up, pulled off his sweater, and Jay and I screened him out the back hallway. Herb was free of love's clutches. The plan worked too well, however. Corinne stopped looking for Herb Staley and fell for Gary Ullin. We chided Gary mercilessly about that over the next few days. Gary just smiled. For him, being stalked by the beautiful brunette Corinne was not such a bad thing.

Paradise befitted its name. It was a fairy-tale place. The sprawling meadows of heather guarded by alpine firs, Rainier looming majestically, the Tatoosh Range forming the sawtooth "Alps" across the small valley, all combined, either in the sun's lustrous light or in the moon's satin glow, to foster love. On any clear summer's night, one could hear the meadows and trees of Paradise speak in giggles and whispers. My voice was among the rest. I had girlfriends up there, but none lasted much past the drive down the hill at the end of the season. The love and bonds born in Paradise broke apart in the world below. The mountain was the glue. Take out the mountain, add rigors of everyday "real" life down in the flat lands, and relationships forged up there melted.

More than one acquaintance ended up married, with a kid close on the heels, as a result of the lure and magic of a moonlit Paradise night. Love up there was, in a word, risky.

   Isn't it always?

# 45  THE SERAC

*A serac is nature's way of sorting out the idiots who linger under them.*

In July 1966 I was teaching a seminar with Lute Jerstad. It was the fourth day, and on the schedule was crevasse rescue and ice climbing. We roped up and swung out on the Cowlitz Glacier below Camp Muir. A portion of the glacier contained a relatively flat section interspersed with several seracs. Seracs are ice pinnacles or towers that spring up among crevasses on a glacier as it moves. We split up into separate groups, and at Lute's direction I took a rope team of two clients over to one of the ice towers. It was approximately fifty feet high with a slight overhang on the downhill side. We laid out our gear of ice screws, slings, and extra carabiners. The lead client started front-pointing with his crampons up the right-hand side of the tower. His teammate took up a belay position, parsing out the rope as the lead climber worked his way methodically off the near-vertical ice wall.

Things were going smoothly. The clients were quick learners. I glanced out briefly at the other teams several hundred feet away. They were making good progress. We were expecting good weather for the summit climb the next day, and we had a strong and well-conditioned clientele on this seminar. It should be a piece of cake, I thought. At that moment I heard a whooshing sound from above, and when I looked up, a large ice block had calved and was coming straight down on top of me. Then everything went black.

Figure 8 Author on upper side of serac near the summit of Rainier.

I don't know how long I was out. It must have been some minutes, because when I woke up I was flat on my back and a ring of faces was looking down at me.

"Are you OK?" A look of concern clouded Jerstad's bearded face.

"I don't know," I heard myself say. They eased me up into a sitting position, and Lute started asking me questions.

"Where are we, George?"

"On Rainier."

"What are we doing?"

"Looking down at me."

"No, no. Okay, what glacier are we on?"

"The Cowlitz. But, Lute," I added, "you're the head guide. If you don't know where you are, we're in big trouble."

Lute scowled, reached down, and pulled me carefully to my feet.

"I've got a headache," I muttered, "and my neck hurts." We called it a day and headed slowly back up to Camp Muir.

Lute handed out some aspirin and told me to lie down on the bunk in the guide hut. "You're not going on the summit climb tomorrow. We've got a strong group, and we can do it without you."

"That's fine with me," I said.

Lute gave me a serious look. "Tonight you can rest, but I'm not going to let you sleep. You were knocked out, which means you've had a head injury. I want to keep you awake tonight to make sure it's not serious. If you still look OK by the time we leave for the summit, you can go to sleep. Then you can head down to Paradise with the clients and me tomorrow afternoon when we break camp after the climb." And that is what transpired...I think.

Weeks later, when I returned to my studies at the

University of Puget Sound, I visited my family dentist. "What have you been up to?" he asked as he peered into my mouth.

When he kindly took his instruments out so I could respond, I said "Just guiding up on Rainier."

"Well, you've got four broken teeth."

So this was a lasting reminder, along with a neck that still hurts on the right side. The best I can figure is that I ducked just enough to receive a glancing blow to the back of my head. It knocked me out, gave me whiplash, and broke four teeth. Not bad, considering the alternative. At least it didn't knock the guardian angel off my shoulder.

# 46  THE SELF-ARREST

*It helps to hold on to the ice axe.*

There was a hard-ridged crust on the snow, even in the afternoon. It was the sastrugi formed by strong cold wind. The Ingraham Glacier would climb well. I never liked the Disappointment Cleaver variation of the standard Muir summit route. Consequently I scouted for a route directly up the Ingraham. I found one. The crux of it was through a steep hourglass ice plug or snow bridge over a large crevasse four hundred feet above camp. We had taken an extra day to acclimatize, and had spent it camped on the Ingraham Flats. Buddy Nye, a Boeing engineer out of Seattle, hand-built a snow saw out of a piece of aircraft aluminum.

"What say we get out of the noisy tents tonight and build an igloo?" Buddy asked.

"If you can build one we'll certainly use it," I said. "None of us got much sleep last night up here." It had been windy.

I was running a private climb of Mount Rainier. The party consisted of old climbing colleagues out of Shelton and Olympia, with a couple of other climbers from Tacoma and Seattle. Most were very experienced. All were in good shape. Nye got to work with his snow saw. He scribed first a large circle. Then he and various assistants, including me, started cutting and laying snow blocks. In two hours, a handsome white igloo spiraled into form. It was done right. The entrance was below floor level and away from the biting wind. A circular sleeping ledge provided ample room. We rolled out our sleeping pads and bags, brought our stoves, food, and eating gear in, and left our packs leaning on the walls outside. Buddy Nye did the honors of poking a vent hole up through the top block in the roof with the shaft of his ice axe.

"Great job, Nye!" I said. "That saw of yours was well-made."

"I can't believe how quiet it is in here," Art Broksis remarked. Art was a Physician's Assistant for Group Health in Tacoma. He was new to the sport, but strong. "That flapping tent we were in last night was like sleeping next to a machine gun."

"This is downright cozy," John Aiken said. John was a lawyer out of Olympia. He and Fred Gentry, also an Olympia attorney, were longtime climbing companions.

## AVOIDING THE SUDDEN STOP

"Our Igloo is snug," Nye said, pulling off his sweater and stuffing it behind his head as a pillow. We lay on our sleeping bags, a happy concentric few. The stoves and our body heat had warmed the air. Art was stirring his hot chocolate.

"I think we've got a good straightforward route up the Ingraham tomorrow," I said. Tonight before we hit the rack, let's get our ropes laid out. It is five o'clock now. Art is the least experienced. I will take him on my rope, with Buddy Nye on the end. The rest of you know your teams and their order in the party?" They nodded.

"Good. In an hour or so, we'll run out the ropes. Put your ice axes down through the loops you're clipping into. That will make things easier to find in the dark. We'll be leaving no later than two thirty in the morning."

Normally I don't sleep prior to a summit climb. This night, however, without the hammering of the wind on nylon it was different. Someone lit a candle lantern and hung it on a string from the igloo's roof. I was out like a light.

Fred Gentry woke me up at one forty-five. We ate breakfast, climbed out of our snow cocoon, donned crampons and ropes, and headed up the hill. Parties from Camp Muir had already passed us and were snaking their way onto lower Disappointment Cleaver, following the standard guide route. Our group, headed by Aiken and Gentry, neatly threaded the big crevasse with the hourglass snow bridge, then zigzagged up the

Ingraham Glacier, past the headwall. We had started later than the Cleaver groups but due to our direct climbing line, ended up ahead of them. Aiken's rope team reached the crater rim at ten o'clock. The weather was clear, but windy and cold. I took Art Broksis over to Columbia Crest and Resister Rock.

"Art, you've done well. Congratulations!" We shook hands and someone took our picture. Art collected a small summit rock and put it in his pack.

Back at the crater rim we all prepared for the descent.

"Look," I said. "We need to watch ourselves going down. The snow is hard, and icy in places. It goes without saying, if you fall, yell it out, and get into a self-arrest fast. Art, do you understand?"

"Yes," he nodded.

At about 13,400 feet, just above the bergschrund, was a steep slab of scoured ice.

"Falling!" Art's voice pierced the wind. His feet went out from under him. I went into a self-arrest, rolling toward my axe-hand, I brought my shoulder into the head of the axe, with the axe-hand over the top, my free hand down the shaft near the point, and my torso leaning against the shaft. Digging my toes in, I levered up on the pick of the axe, forcing it down into the hard snow. The rope came taught, and pulled hard on my waist. It pulled harder. I was now holding Art's entire body weight on my arrest. Why didn't he stop himself? I glanced down. Broksis was in a self-arrest position. The only problem was that his ice axe was stuck in the snow ten feet above his head. He'd completely lost his axe.

"Art, what the hell's going on?"

"I lost my axe," he said sheepishly as he got up and retrieved it.

"I see that. Why didn't you have your wrist loop on?"

"I took it off to take a picture and forgot to put it back on."

"OK, do you get the picture on how the self-arrest works? You need an ice axe to do it, remember?"

"Yes, my hand slipped off the head." Art carefully put on his wrist loop and started walking. A few dozen feet later he fell again. This time he flipped neatly into a proper self-arrest position. We both did.

"That's the way, Art, good! Now keep one eye on yourself and the other on Buddy down in front of you."

Art fell, and self-arrested, several more times before we arrived back on the Ingraham Flats and our Igloo. But he had it down pat by them. So did I—roll into the head of the axe, dig the toes in wide, and lever up on the shaft and torso. Keep the shoulder tucked up next to the pick and drive the pick down with all your weight and strength. That is how a sudden stop is survived on snow. And that is how we walked away from another good climb of Mount Rainier.

## 47   Death in the Basin

*Cinemas of sentience and sorrow.*

At three in the afternoon on June 15, 1967, RGS manager Jack Melill walked into the store and rental facility in The DUB. "A ranger just told me that there's been an accident," he said. We stopped our work behind the counter.

"Do they need us?" John Rutter asked.

"Yes, but we have to wait for more information. Three members of a family that rented boots from us this morning are missing—a mother and two daughters. The father walked into the ranger station carrying his four-year-old son, who had a head injury. He said that his son fell into a creek under the snow over in Edith Creek Basin. The father worked his way down to retrieve his son, but when he brought his son out, he said he couldn't find his wife and two daughters."

"I remember them," I said. "I rented boots to them this morning. They said they were going to hike to the ice caves." I looked at the rental register. "It was Melvin Louden and his family."

Melill nodded. "The Louden boy is being transported to the hospital in Tacoma. He had a bad head injury. Melvin, the dad, is at the ranger station being debriefed. When we get a green light from the rangers, we'll start looking for the rest of the family. Get ready."

John Rutter, Jay Sprenger, Jack Hebert, and I grabbed our packs and the first-aid kits. We also packed our headlights. It was already five o'clock. It would be dark soon.

A ranger walked in and briefed us. "We are going to have to look for Melvin's wife and two daughters. He's in shock and can't go with us. That means we'll have to search most of the Edith Creek Basin. All he knows is that he was on the basin trail walking back toward the inn when he noticed the old Paradise Road farther down. He decided to take the family down to the road by way of a snow gully. The gully got steep and his son slipped and fell into a snow hole with a creek running under it."

The night was spent looking. As dawn broke the next day, one of the searchers saw scrape marks on the snow above a waterfall. Twenty feet below, where the falls ran back under the snow, a pair of dark glasses was spotted laying on the lip above the tunnel. The guide-ranger rescue party assembled there. A ranger was roped up and belayed down into the tunnel and freezing water. A few minutes later he came back. "The mother is down there," he said, shivering. "She's dead." We pulled an akja up next to the cave. Another ranger in rain gear went down with an extra rope. He emerged ten minutes later, thoroughly chilled.

"The mom is hooked up. I saw the body of one of her daughters. She's in a pool about ten feet below the mom." We pulled Phyllis Louden's body out and put her in the akja. Another rain-geared ranger went down. We retrieved the small body of Kelly Louden. Rangers tried to search lower under the falls but it was too cold and dangerous to continue.

Two days later, a U.S. Navy scuba diver recovered the second young daughter, Karen Louden. She was lodged eighty feet down, wedged between the narrowing snow and the stream.

In one sunny afternoon, a family out for a hike around Paradise was virtually wiped out. Three were dead. Mark, the little boy with the head injury, was operated on and survived. We conferred with the rangers trying to piece together the sequence of events. It was concluded that when Melvin was extracting his son from the cave, his wife, holding her daughters' hands, had slipped; they had been swept over the falls and past Melvin without his knowing it. The tumbling water drowned out any sounds of the fall. When he climbed up out of the hole with his injured son, his wife and daughters had disappeared. He didn't notice Phyllis's dark glasses laying in the snow above the tunnel. They had spun off and landed there during her fall.

Signs in the park urge hikers to stay on the trails. Snow banks over streams are one of the reasons for them.

Just the day before I had rented hiking boots to the Louden family. They had been excited and enthusiastic to hike out and enjoy the trails and terrain around Paradise, as so many thousands do every summer. Yet it was the lot of the mother and two daughters that led them to quick and tragic deaths. I continued to dream them in two cinematic scenes. In the first they were breathing, upright, and joyful; and in the second they were cold, limp, and lifeless. The scenes blended instantly together without fading, demarcation, or reason. One moment they were here, and the next there was only the movie to animate them. I grieved.

# 48 THE DISAPPOINTMENT

*Sweating it out on the Cleaver.*

Disappointment Cleaver is a large rock ridge that divides the Ingraham and Emmons Glaciers. It is the "standard" route on a climb of Mount Rainier from Camp Muir. It is also dangerous.

"Joe, coil up your rope mate. You're leaving Sarah exposed to rockfall. Now, is everyone ready? We've just climbed onto the lower end of Disappointment Cleaver. Keep your left hand on the fixed line. As you can see, there's a cliff right below us. It runs into a very big hole in the glacier. So stay bunched together. We can't afford to get strung out here because we will be zig-zagging up this thing on the rocks. If we get too much distance between each other the climbers on top will be knocking rocks down on those below. All the rock here is shifting and loose. There is a tiny switchback trail that's been kicked in. Stay on it. If a rock moves or is kicked loose by the guy in front of you, just reach down and stop it before it can get moving and hurt someone. If you can't stop it yell 'Rock!' Got it?" Even in the darkness I could tell the clients' eyes were wide. There were a few tentative nods. "OK, let's go."

The crunch and ping of crampons and ice axes hitting rock were the only sounds. Clients, chattering away on the Ingraham Glacier minutes before, were now silent on the Cleaver. Disappointment did that to climbers. Once on its steep, exposed slopes, the game of climbing Rainier was no longer one. I heard a scuffing and a rock dislodged. I looked back to see that a client had reached down and checked its roll into those below. "Good job, Ken," I said. "Hold your hand on it for a moment. Everyone, did you see what Ken just did to stop the rock? When that happens, just do what Ken did." I nodded to Ken and he carefully lifted his hand off the rock. We moved on.

About five hundred vertical feet up the Cleaver we traversed to the left to a steep snowfield. There were no fixed ropes on this section, which ran to the Cleaver's top at over 12,000 feet, but the trail was well-defined with good footholds. "We're entering the snowfield now, folks," I said. "Just like we practiced in the snow school yesterday, as each climber reaches the snow, the climber in back waits, lets the rope uncoil as the front man climbs, and so on, until we're all spread out with no

## AVOIDING THE SUDDEN STOP

coils, and no slack in the rope, OK?" The banging of axes against rocks subsided into the softer sounds of axe and crampon points biting into hard snow. It was here that the rest step sorted out the group. Those who were in shape and used it, had enough energy to reach the summit. Those who weren't in shape or scrambled instead of relying on rhythm and balance, would be left in sleeping bags at the top of the Cleaver to await the party's return. Hence the name, Disappointment Cleaver.

It was now getting light enough to turn off my headlamp. I turned and paused for a moment. Climbers below were spaced out neatly like beads on a string. Dave Stelling was guiding the last rope, and I could see his headlamp winking as he climbed. Usually he turned it off by now unless there was a problem client he needed to keep an eye on. Probably Andy, I thought. Andy was not in the best shape and was tentative on the self-arrest practice in the snow school he was in two days ago. Especially the part where he had to self-arrest when sliding head down on his back. That grabs a lot of clients and is normal; but Andy was not just anxious. I sensed that he was wrestling a demon—a deep down fear—acrophobia. Stelling had noticed this too, and we had discussed it.

"Andy's really tight," Dave said during the school. That was code for "fearful."

"I agree, Dave," I said. "I think we should drop him from the summit list."

"I do too, but," Stelling paused. "You know what's going to happen. It will probably get nixed. They'll tell us to take him anyway."

And that's what had happened. Dave and I had hoped that Andy would crap out at Camp Muir but he didn't. He dogged his way up to high camp—not pretty, but he did it—to his credit. Dave then talked privately with Andy the night before the climb:

"Andy, do you think you're really ready to climb this thing?" Stelling said. Without waiting for an answer, he added, "I know you paid good money for this climb, but I can talk with the RGS manager, and see if we can refund at least part of your fee. You're not in peak condition, and you've struggled. Are you having anxiety about this trip? If you are, that's totally understandable. There's no problem at all if you stay here in camp. You can sleep in and have a good hot breakfast and lunch."

"No," Andy said, looking down. "I want to do the climb." Stelling shrugged and said, "OK, Andy."

At the top of the Cleaver I coiled in my rope team and sat down on my pack. The sun was just rising to a clear day. The big light beacon at the Moses Lake Airfield many miles to the east had turned off. Its slow, flashing rotation was a night friend—a sign, that way off somewhere there was life and civilization. When climbing the Cleaver I would catch myself synchronizing my climbing to its rotation. Flash, step, breathe, flash, step, breathe. Slow, steady, flash, step, breathe. It was the perfect visual metronome.

## AVOIDING THE SUDDEN STOP

"Sit down on your packs, and break out your lunches," I said to arriving clients. This is the first big rest stop. You've earned it."

The top of Disappointment merged flat with the glaciers coursing around it. The level area of the top was about the size of a couple of parking spaces. So situated, it was the last safe location to leave a struggling client. Stelling was slowly bringing up the rear with Andy. I unslung and unrolled the foam ground pad and extra sleeping bag from the bottom of my Kelty. I could see that Andy couldn't go the distance.

Dave, stopped beside me and coiled in Andy and the rest of his rope team. He saw my pad and bag and nodded. "This is as far as Andy goes."

"Andy, how are you doing?" Stelling said. Andy was breathing so hard that he couldn't answer. He stood, bending over, using his ice axe as a prop. "We are going to have to leave you here," Dave continued. Let's get your crampons off and into the sleeping bag here." This time there was no resistance. Andy crawled in.

"You have plenty of water and food, Andy."

"Yes." Andy was barely audible.

"All you need to do is rest here. Get some sleep, and we'll be back in a few hours to pick you up to go back to Muir, OK?"

"Yes."

Stelling and I walked out of earshot of Andy and the rest of the clients.

"There's nothing physically wrong with Andy," Dave

said. "He's just beat. He was really tight, using up way too much energy."

"He's fearful and won't admit it," I said.

"Yeah, we'll have to watch him on the way down," Dave concurred.

The rest of the party was strong. Our RGS party summited and was back down at the top of Disappointment in five hours. We roped Andy back in and started down the Cleaver's snowfield. In the first rope length he stopped and sat down.

"What's the matter Andy?" Dave stooped down to look at him. Andy sat frozen, his face catatonic. He didn't respond.

"I think Andy's acrophobic," I said. "Andy! Get up!" Dave and I pulled him to his feet.

"I can't go down!" Andy blurted out. I motioned Dave aside.

"This is serious. We have to get him to walk. He looks out to the horizon and won't look down at his feet, because when he does he sees the exposure below him and it freezes him up," I said. "He must have been able to control his fear on the way up because he was facing into the hill. Now that he's facing out he's overcome."

"What'll we do? I've never seen this before."

"We will have to walk Andy down. Let's rearrange our rope teams. Put John on the tail end of my rope in the anchor position. He's strong and has prior climbing experience. I will take the lead and short-rope Andy from the right side. I grabbed Andy's prusik sling tied next to him on his rope and snapped the free end into my waist with a carabiner. Put Norman on the front end of your rope. He's a former semi-pro football player, and is tough and strong."

Norman took Andy's left side and I took the right. Andy didn't say much. He was rigid, like a rusted robot. Slowly, supported by Norman and me, we worked Andy down the snowfield and onto the rocky flank of the lower Cleaver. Once in a while Andy would moan quietly. I tried to divert him with constant chatter.

"Andy good, you're moving. Take a little longer step. Don't look out anywhere—only at your feet. Concentrate on your feet. Don't worry, we'll be off this thing and down on the Ingraham Flats in no time." That wasn't true, but it sounded good to me. It took our party two and a half hours to descend Disappointment Cleaver. But we did—safely. When we finally made to flatter terrain on the glacier, Andy perked up. I was proud of him and told him so; but by the time Stelling and I got the party back to Camp Muir we were beat. As we packed up to go back to Paradise, Stelling and I talked.

"That was a bitch of a situation," Dave said. "We're lucky we had good weather and a strong party. Our resources were strained with having just one client go sideways. We're climbing here at RGS with too thin a margin," he said. "We need more authority to disqualify questionable clients. And that damned Cleaver—every time I get on that thing with clients it gives me the willies. You and I have had so many close calls on it with parties." He paused. "Do you think it's dangerous?"

"Yes, I've never liked it. I'd prefer staying on the Ingraham Glacier instead, but Disappointment has been adopted as the standard route because it gives you fifteen hundred vertical feet on a trail that is relatively unchanging. Any other route on the hill changes constantly, and takes up time resetting the trail when the snow bridges go out," I said. "But I've never like Disappointment. It's relentlessly steep and exposed."

Three weeks later, Dave Stelling quit guiding at the RGS. He and I worked well together. It took twelve years to confirm our observations. In 1980, the Disappointment Cleaver route would witness the greatest tragedy in U.S. mountaineering history. Eleven climbers on a guided climb were swept away in an avalanche. Their bodies were never recovered. Sudden stops sometimes end that way on big mountains.

## 49 THE HUMMINGBIRD

*If only I could follow him.*

We were climbing down from the summit of Mount Rainier. It was a hot day, about one o'clock in the afternoon, and our rope teams were just getting ready to cross the snow-bridged bergschrund at about 13,300 feet. Except for the sounds of clients banging ice axes against their snow-clogged crampons, all was silent. The air was dead calm. The vast, broken Ingraham Glacier curved majestically out of sight below my feet. I glanced up at the horizon, and the sight of a beautiful green hummingbird caused me to freeze in midstride. The lack of ambient sound amplified the buzz of the bird's wings. It met me precisely at eye level, looking me over. As I overcame the shock of this unexpected encounter, it dawned on me that the small iridescent bird must have thought that the bright red felt hat I was wearing was a succulent flower. In the few seconds that it took for us to discern each other, the bird with the blurring wings realized that it was not looking at a flower at all, but at a tired young climber with dark glasses for eyes and a face slathered in suntan lotion. It was certainly also obvious that I smelled nothing like a flower. Armed with that revelation, the stunning green body, topped with a mottled tan neck ring and a dark head with bright pinpoint eyes—and the thunderous buzz that accompanied it—was gone.

Why the hummingbird was up at such high altitudes was a mystery. Perhaps it was there to evade the lowland heat of a hot summers' day. Perhaps the altitude affected its brain, the same way it affected my clients' and mine up here high on Rainier. But at that moment, as I watched the bird fly away, I sorely envied its fast and efficient mode of transport. My clients and I slogged wearily down. We all longed to be back among the flowers and the hummingbirds—among the green trees and meadows—off the hill.

I was off the hill for good in the summer of 1968. I thought that maybe someday I'd be back up at the RGS. Instead, I finished school, got married, and went off to complete my Air Force obligation to fight a war. It would be years before I returned to the Northwest and the mountains, and in that time life for me took a different trajectory. I have come to understand that's how

## AVOIDING THE SUDDEN STOP

life is—trajectories, some volitional, some involuntary, but always seeking—like a hummingbird.

# 50 Goodbye Old Saint

*"The earth is flattening out over its axis. The shoreline is sinking away. Nothing, it seems, has ever happened here. History becomes geology." —Colin Thubron*

The phone rang incessantly. It was Sunday, May 18th 1980, and my goal was to sleep in. That quashed, I finally rolled over and picked up the handset.

"Have you heard the news?" My mom's voice forced its way into my head.

"No, mom, what?"

"Mount Saint Helens has erupted. It's all over the news, and we heard the boom all the way over here at Hoodsport at around eight o'clock this morning." Hoodsport, on Hood Canal, was a crow's flight of one hundred twenty miles from the mountain.

"Are you sure you heard it?" I answered, my grogginess now replaced by doubt.

"Yes! Look out the window."

"OK, mom, I'll look and call you back" I said.

The view out of the apartment window took my breath away. It was now ten o'clock, but looked like midnight. But rather than the black of night, the world was a deep dark gray. The ash from Saint Helens was at my door. I called mom back.

"This is unbelievable, mom! It is so dark out there I can't even see my car in the parking lot. There is at least four inches of ash here."

"Really?" Mom said, surprised "We've had no ash here yet."

Figure 9 BFH climbing away on the North slopes of Saint Helens, 1961. The slopes no longer exist.

With the eruption, the mountain I'd known so well

and grown up on, was gone, its rocks and glaciers seared into vast denuded surroundings, and launched up into the stratosphere, caught by the western jet stream, and deposited in angry gray layers stretching from my window to the Midwestern states.

"I wonder if the ash hit Shelton," I said, breaking into my own thoughts.

"Why don't you call your dad and ask him?" mom replied. We rang off and I called BFH.

"We've got a trace of it here," he said. "My barograph recorded the blast's pressure wave here at about 0820. It was a big one." We talked a few more minutes and hung up. On a hunch I dug out my calendar. Sure enough, precisely one year ago on May 18th 1979, BFH, our Shelton climbing group, and I had climbed Saint Helens. On the way down we noticed steam vents had appeared on the flank of the mountain where they'd never been seen before. Then, in the next geologic half heartbeat, the old Saint Helens, the beautiful cone that graced my eye in the many summer days when I gazed toward the southern horizon from the doorstep of the guide hut at Camp Muir, was gone. All that remained was its empty base, looking like the socket of a broken tooth. I reflected that I'd climbed the mountain between fifteen to twenty times. Every trip demanded and received my respect, and filled me out as a climber and a guide. In my early years it challenged every fiber, taught me balance, tolerance to exposure, and patient persistence. Above all, it taught me about me. The "Old

Saint" was a perennial teacher. It got into my head and lives on there.

The passing of Saint Helens coincided with a watershed in my life. This big glaciered volcano of my youth had seemed immutable, but the Old Saint had shown me otherwise. It lives its moments as I live mine. It rises and falls to its own grinding, airy rhythms—like Rainier and all other grand god-stones called mountains. They inexorably move on, just as we must.

# Conclusion

*Look past yourself into the mountains, and you will find what you left behind.*

My salad days of youth, climbing, and guiding are finished. Following my time in the US Air Force and law school under the GI Bill, I did not go back to practice law with my father in Shelton, where he ultimately lawyered for fifty-seven years. As much as I loved and admired BFH, I needed to seek a path other than under his aegis. I became a special agent with the FBI and spent twenty-two years there. I enjoyed the cases and colleagues, but that time of my life was urban. I needed rural. I wanted to get back to the Northwest, BFH, my mom and family, and most of all, the mountains. I now live in the softer hills of Oregon on eight acres of Chehalem Mountain. There, I plant my trees, build trails, fish in my trout pond, and live life rural. I have come home.

But it was in the mountains, at a vulnerable young age, trying to avoid the sudden stop that I learned and pushed my inner limits. It was there that I gained perspective on my place in the world. It was where I controlled fear, helped others control it, and thrilled at the joys of my own and others' accomplishments at Mount Rainier and points beyond. It was where I grew up. It was where I got the measure of myself. A life that has been mountain-stamped is uniquely validated. In every endeavor ever after in the "flat lands," it was the inculcation of resolve and inner toughness, of perspectives of myself and others that stood me well—especially in my career as a special agent of the FBI.

To the mountains we are nothing special, but to ourselves we are, because we were in them. We were there. And while there, we were able to look past ourselves, however fleetingly, and find what we left behind.

The life circles of some of my fellow colleagues, family members, and mountaineers, who shared my early life in the mountains and hills of the Northwest are encapsulated below. So far as I am aware, all are either living happy or finally died happy. That is a summit in itself.

Frank Maranville, a chemist at Rayonier Inc. in Shelton, died of cancer in 2001 at eighty-two.

Louis Stur died in a fall on a peak in his beloved Idaho, age sixty-four.

Gary Ullin died in an avalanche in the Pamir Mountains in 1974, age thirty-one.

## AVOIDING THE SUDDEN STOP

Catherine Heuston and Tom Needham live in Gilbert, Arizona, and hike there. Tom retired as a bank executive. Catherine taught English and German in local schools.

Mary Heuston worked for the State of Washington Liquor Control Commission at Olympia and is now retired, remarried, and content.

Jerry Shimek became a teacher in Tacoma public schools, and retired after thirty years.

Bob Jeffery, thanks to Catherine and her knot, went to Stanford, became a professor, and is now retired.

Lute Jerstad died of a heart attack in 1998, on Kala Patthar Peak, Nepal. He was sixty one.

My mother, Ruth, died in 2003, at age eighty five. BFH and mom were divorced in 1970, and both remarried into happy relationships.

My father died of cancer in 2008, age ninety four. The old "vintage climber" was a brilliant attorney, and a good husband in his second marriage. Relentless in his goals, a fighter, on the mountain, in the court room, and at home, he was a man who knew how to get his way and usually did. That did not help in his relationship with mom. She wanted things her way, too. There was little compromise between them. BFH was strict, "old school." I know he loved me but he was unable to express it in direct terms. I am at peace with him, and have been since I gained self-confidence and perspective by going my own way in life. It was my experiences at the Rainier Guide Service, which provided the catalyst to break away. I became my father's equal. And as an equal, the relationship between father and son was able to blossom into a love enhanced by true friendship. I, along with my sons, Eric, Scott, Wesley, and Eric's wife, Andrea, deposited his ashes on Mount Rainier at the place of his choosing. BFH chose well.

My Shoulder Angel, paternal grandmother Slava Balabanoff Heuston, was killed June 24th, 1950 on Northwest Flight 2501, along with my grandfather Ben, and all the other fifty-six souls on board. I was not yet two years old when she died, but my sisters claimed she loved me more than they—that "George was the apple of her eye," and that she held me constantly. It was traditional in Bulgarian families to favor sons and grandsons; and I know she favors me to this day, always at my shoulder. She did yeoman service for me when I climbed, and when her son, BFH, walked me occasionally into harm's way. When I guided I wore the thick navy blue hand-made woolen vest she had knitted for my dad way back in the 1920s. The grandmother I never knew in life, I have come to know in her passing. I have kept her close, and continue to thank her and the Good Lord for watching out for me in subsequent journeys through the military, the FBI, and now through the more benign repose of a pleasant retirement.

So run life's streams. I was fortunate to be able to drink from them, in those early days, when they ran pure, clear, and cold.

# Epilogue

*Moonlight to Muir*

Decades later I hiked to Camp Muir with my sons Eric, Scott, and Wesley. We walked at night. Between Alta Vista and Panorama rose a large blood-red moon.

"Dad, there's a forest fire beyond the ridge," Wesley said.

"No, son, it is just the bright moon rising."

It turned gradually yellow as it climbed above the eastern horizon. Short trail sections on Pan required occasional squibs from headlamps as the dark western rocks were shadowed. In contrast, the entirety of the Kautz summit route and the Nisqually Glacier were bathed in moonlight. They reflected a textured dreamscape of crevasses, sleeping ice walls, and towering rock cleavers. The impression was of walking through a watercolor, with brushstrokes yielding mysterious indistinct lines. The canvass was a soft night and a caressing northeast breeze.

Cresting Panorama Point brought our party out of the shadows for good. We crossed Pebble Creek and the two small snow cirques forming its north edge. We were gaining one thousand feet an hour. Breaks were short due to the coolness of the night. We lolled along the broad Muir snowfields with the moon. Another break at Moon Rocks, and we arrived at Camp Muir at four in the morning. The old Guide Hut stood silent, padlocked on the outside. The public hut was closed but occupied. We walked quietly. A cluster of tents was nestled on the Cowlitz Glacier a few feet off the scree.

I looked up along the Cowlitz, pointing out to my sons the fine dark ribbon of the summit route across the Cowlitz and up talus slopes to Cathedral Gap, where it disappeared onto the Ingraham Glacier. I pointed out the twinkling headlamps of climbers near the top of Disappointment Cleaver. They were so far away and swallowed by the night. My sons and I stood, watched, and listened. There was no sound but the embracing white noise formed by air coping with sheer distance and mass. It was palpable.

Wesley's Suunto watch registered twenty eight degrees Fahrenheit. There was no wind. We settled down in the rocks to wait out the dawn. My nylon trail boots were wet from an unplanned dip into Pebble Creek. Consequently, my feet were only cold enough to keep me awake. This was well. The mellowing views whispered to be seen. Above, Gibraltar slept, standing silent guard over the upper Cowlitz. I told my sons of my climbs on its rubbled ledges, and of those long, long ago when the first guides and clients climbed them. The mind's ear could discern the scraping of hobnailed boots and the knocking of alpenstocks among the rocks.

As the sky lightened the predawn, I noticed a large snow platform dug into the Cowlitz adjacent to the Guide Hut. Several fifty gallon black barrels sat there with snow shovels resting against them. These black barrels melted snow into fresh water for the guides and clients. The sun rose and cast a long Mount Rainier shadow westward over low valley mists, colored pink and violet. I sat with my sons, as BFH had sat with me, before my first climb of Rainier, and as Gary Ullin and I had sat looking out years ago when we decided to do the night climb. It was still.

The circles of life touched in the moment—and were filled.

# Glossary

*Alpenstock:* A long wooden pole with an iron spike at the bottom and a curved spike at the top, used by climbers prior to the advent of the ice axe.

*Belay:* A means of protecting a roped-in moving climber where the non-moving climber (belayer) pays the rope through or around a friction-generating surface to arrest a fall. The surface may be the belayer's body, or the boot and shaft of his anchored ice axe, or a specific mechanical belay device.

*Bergschrund:* A large crevasse at the upper end of a glacier.

*Bivouac:* A temporary shelter or camp.

*Bowline:* A reliable and ancient maritime and climbing knot used to tie a loop into a rope.

*Bollard:* A mound of snow or ice, with a horseshoe shaped groove cut around it to which a fixed or anchoring rope is attached.

*Bulgari:* A technique of crevasse rescue where the victim steps up in belayed rope loops, or stirrups. As the victim raises his feet, belayers above take in the slack and hold the rope so the victim can step up. Each foot is successively belayed in this fashion, allowing the victim to "climb" out of the crevasse.

*Buttress:* A large rock formation or outcrop on a mountain, flanked by gullies.

*Carabiner:* A strong metal link with a spring-hinged opening or "gate," used for clipping into rope or other climbing gear.

*Cerebral edema:* An excess accumulation of fluid in the brain of a climber induced by higher altitudes. It can be swiftly fatal.

*Cirque:* A steep amphitheater at the head of a valley.

*Clown white:* A pasty white zinc oxide cream applied as sunscreen, usually to the face.

*Cornice:* A wind-shaped overhang of snow or ice on a ridge.

*Couloir:* A chute or gully.

*Crampons:* A set of metal spikes that attach to the soles of climbing boots for traction on snow or ice.

*Crevasse:* A crack or rift in a glacier.

*Dulfersitz:* A rope friction rappel which passes through a climber's legs, around a hip, over the opposite shoulder, and is controlled by the hand from that opposite shoulder.

*Fall line:* The vertical line of a slope.

*Fisherman's knot:* A knot used to tie two rope ends

together.

*Frostbite:* Frozen tissue.

*Gaiters:* Protective coverings worn over the top of climbing boots to keep out water, snow, and debris.

*Glacier:* A river of ice and snow.

*Glissade:* A controlled slide on snow, using the ice axe's shaft as a brake. It is usually done sitting, but may be done standing as well.

*Goldline rope:* A three-strand "laid" or "twisted" nylon rope that revolutionized climbing by being able to bear high-impact loads. Older natural-fiber ropes were not nearly as reliable, and tended to break under high dynamic or static loads.

*Headband:* AKA, "Ear Brassiere," is a warm fabric band worn around the head to protect the ears from the cold.

*Hobnail boot:* A climbing boot whose soles are studded with short blunted nails to increase traction and decrease wear on the soles.

*Ice Axe:* A climbing tool with a metal head composed of an adz, or blade, and a pick, and a shaft. It is used for balance, to arrest falls, and for chopping steps or handholds in snow or ice.

*Ice screw:* A metal piton anchor with a screw shaft used as an anchor in hard snow or ice.

*Knickers:* Loose, baggy pants gathered at the knee, that allowed for free leg and knee movement prior to the advent of stretch fabrics.

*Knicker socks:* Long woolen socks held up by the

gathered or fastened end of the knicker pants below the knee.

*Lead climber:* The first ascender and route finder in a climbing party.

*Leader fall:* A fall by the lead climber ascending, or by the anchoring climber descending on a rope team. A "leader fall" plummets twice the distance of the rope between the next climber on the rope team, and is thus especially dangerous.

*Piton:* A metal anchor spike with an eye at the blunt end to attach a carabiner or runner.

*Prusik:* A one-way knot tied into slings on a climbing rope to enable a climber to ascend the rope.

*Quonset hut:* A semicircular prefabricated metal building.

*Rappel:* A controlled means of descending a vertical face on a rope anchored from above.

*Rest step:* A means of climbing to rest and sustain muscle strength in the legs.

*Rime ice:* Ice patterns and icicles formed on rock or other surfaces by cold blowing fog.

*Runner:* A sling attached to a piton. A carabiner is then clipped into the sling.

*Sastrugi:* Erosion formations and grooves in snow formed by wind.

*Self-arrest:* A means of stopping (arresting) a fall by use of an ice axe.

*Serac:* An ice tower extruded upward by the downward flow of a glacier.

## AVOIDING THE SUDDEN STOP

*Sling:* Nylon webbing, stitched or tied.

*Spindrift:* Small particles of snow or ice spun and swirled by the wind.

*Swami belt:* A flat nylon webbing, or rope, tied around a climber's waist. A carabiner is then used to clip into the main climbing rope.

*Tricouni boot:* A climbing boot from the turn of the 20th century, consisting of small metal teeth embedded in the soles to improve traction on snow and ice.

*Tumpline:* A sling running from the top of a backpack to the climber's forehead to assist in bearing the load.

# Photo Credits

Part 1 - Base Camp

1. By B.F. Heuston
2. By B.F. Heuston
3. By Frank Maranville
4. By B.F. Heuston
5. By B.F. Heuston
6. By B.F. Heuston
7. By Frank Maranville
8. By Frank Willard
9. By B.F. Heuston
10. By Frank Maranville
11. By B.F. Heuston
12. By B.F. Heuston
13. By Jerry Shimek
14. By Jerry Shimek
15. By Jerry Shimek

16. By Jerry Shimek
17. By G.Z. Heuston
18. By B.F. Heuston
19. By G.Z. Heuston
20. By G.Z. Heuston
21. By B.F. Heuston
22. By Tim Pinkney
23. By Tim Pinkney
24. By B.F. Heuston

Part 2 - High Camp

1. By G.Z. Heuston
2. By G.Z. Heuston
3. By G.Z. Heuston
4. By Fred Gentry
5. By B.F. Heuston
6. By G.Z. Heuston
7. By TripAdvisor.com
8. By Norm Bishop
9. By Jerry Shimek

# ABOUT THE AUTHOR

George Zell Heuston grew up in the woods and mountains near his hometown of Shelton, Washington, on the Olympic Peninsula. Mentored by his father, a vintage Northwest mountaineer, George began climbing at age seven, in the days of wooden ice axes and stiff braided nylon ropes. Throughout his youth, he climbed all the major peaks in the Olympics and Cascades. His experience culminated with three memorable summers of guiding on Mount Rainier in the mid-1960s. During this time the Vietnam War was gaining momentum, and following graduation from the University of Puget Sound with a B.A. in history, he served four years as an intelligence officer in the U.S. Air Force, targeting B-52 airstrikes in Vietnam. Following his Air Force tour, George obtained a Juris Doctor law degree from Seattle University School of Law under the G.I. Bill. Thereafter, George Zell Heuston was sworn in as a Special Agent of the FBI. He spent 22 years as a special agent in the Seattle, Las Vegas, San Francisco, and Portland FBI field offices. He retired in 2002 to work as a Project Manager for the Hillsboro Police Department, Oregon. Following diagnosis of prostate cancer and successful surgery, George retired a second time from HPD in 2009. He wrote a weekly news column for the Hillsboro Argus and OregonLive on cyber-related crime and security issues from 2002-2012. George Zell Heuston now resides on a mountain near Newberg, Oregon, with his wife Paula, dogs, cats, chickens, ducks, and a four-mountain Cascade view: Mount Hood, Mount Adams, Mount Saint Helens, and Mount Rainier. In the repose of an active retirement, George Zell Heuston has ample time to review his days of active mountaineering. He has realized that the value of those experiences, which seemed so distant when he was working, have now come flooding back with clarity nuanced by perspective. It is his objective to share those experiences in his writing.

Made in the USA
San Bernardino, CA
22 February 2015